Baby Gorilla

By Daniel Gundert

ISBN Paperback: 979-8-89576-137-3
ISBN Hardback: 979-8-89576-138-0

Published by:

Table of Contents

baby gorilla

/ˈbeɪ.bi gəˈrɪ.lə/ **noun**

A term of affection for someone in a raw stage of growth—strong, sensitive, and not yet aware of their own power. Used between parent and child, it describes a bond where fierce love meets emotional volatility, and where transformation is forged through care, consistency, and a shared struggle. In rare cases, the term is mutual—each shaping the other's becoming.

chalk up

/ ʧɔːk ʌp/ **verb phrase**

---

1 *To coat the hands before attempting something challenging. A quiet ritual of readiness. Preparation for the grip, and to mark the start of something that matters.* **2** *To categorize or frame a fall, mistake, or wrongdoing, with the intention of seeking transformation via the lessons learned, e.g., "chalk it up to experience."*

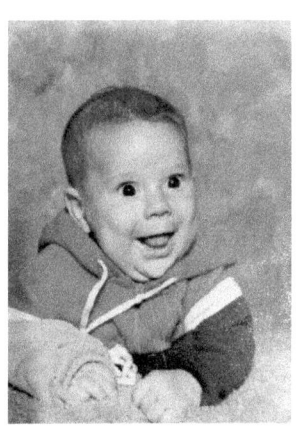

There was a time I didn't think I'd live past thirty. A time when I thought my story would end on a city bus, on the floor of a hospital, in a jail cell, or worse. But here I am—alive, clear-eyed, and filled with more love than I ever imagined a human heart could hold. Sometimes my heart hurts from an abundance of gratitude.

Over the past few years, I've been working on this book, *Baby Gorilla*. It's a memoir about addiction, recovery, and rebuilding. It's also about becoming a father, a husband, a leader, and a man who's learned—slowly and stubbornly— how to show up for life. I didn't write this to shock or impress. I wrote it because I believe our *mess*, with *age*, can become our *message*—if we're willing to tell the truth.

The truth.

I'll make a deal with you: Stick with me and I'll be honest on all fronts, including the salacious and the audacious, the disgraceful and the discoveries; not just the lows but also the recoveries and the possibilities, and not just the possibilities for me but for *all* of us.

Before I was a business owner or a dad of five, I was a scared, angry, addicted young man who didn't think he was worth saving, who didn't think life was worth staying for. I've let people down. I've vanished from the lives of those who loved me. I've done things I'm not proud of. But I've also clawed my way back—through recovery, through humility, and through a relentless commitment to doing better. I've been sober since 2020, and today, I run Gyminny Kids, an 8-figure gymnastics business with over 6,000 weekly students, four locations, and a team of 100-plus professionals I believe in. It's more than a gym—it's a place where kids, coaches, and families become who they're meant to be, including me.

This book isn't a résumé. It's not a redemption campaign or a glossy highlight reel. It's scar tissue. It's memory, as I experienced it: foggy, fragile, sometimes painful, and sometimes distasteful. Some characters have been merged for the sake of narrative flow, and some moments compressed. But the truth—the emotional truth—is all here.

If you've known me in real life, some of what's in these pages may surprise you. And if you're part of this story—whether we shared a season, a struggle, a second chance, or a simple moment of grace—know this: I'm grateful. You helped bring me here.

To the families who've trusted us at Gyminny Kids, thank you. I know this story may feel personal to you as well. And I want you to know that what we teach—confidence, resilience, character—didn't come from textbooks; it came from lived experience; the rough and tumble of life, falling hard and learning how to get back up.

To those still in the thick of it—still wrestling with shame, fighting for one good day—I see you. I've been there. This book is for you. You're not alone, and it's not too late. It's *never* too late.

And to my daughter Finley—my Baby Gorilla—you struck a chord where no one else did. You've seen me at my worst and loved me anyway. There are no words that I can find that adequately express my gratitude for your piercing of my soul, like a hypodermic syringe injecting innocence, purpose, responsibility, and love into the heart of my heart.

This is the story of how my baby gorilla broke my fever, and how I built a life worth staying for.

Thank you for letting me share it.

Ok, let's chalk up.

~ Daniel Gundert

false start

/fɔːls staːt / **noun**

---

1. A premature takeoff. 2. When a body initiates motion before receiving the official signal, or the soul is ready. 3, An attempt begun too soon, before the signal, before alignment, before the mind catches up to the feet. 4. A sprint toward worthiness, driven by fire, fear, or the need to escape stillness.

Chapter 1

springboard

/sprɪŋˌbɔːd/ **noun**

A raised platform designed and used to create upward momentum and often positioned just before a leap into the unknown.

"Why didn't my baby gorilla put me to bed last night, like you promised?"

The question was simple enough. The answer, however, was more complex. There was no answer; not a good one, at least.

Finley lay next to me, her face inches from mine. She looked magical and dreamy, illuminated by what seemed to be beams of golden light from another glorious San Diego sunrise that streamed through our glass sliding doors into our home.

"Hi, baby girl."

I'd said this to her once when she was a toddler. We had a thing for gorillas, and she'd misheard me and thought I'd called her "baby gorilla." We laughed so hard, and the term stuck. From then on, she was my "baby gorilla," and I was hers. From then on, her baby gorilla tucked her in.

But not last night, he didn't, nor the night before, nor the night before that. So, her question was a fair one; why hadn't her baby gorilla tucked her in?

Just moments earlier, I'd heard my now-six-year-old daughter come into the living room, where I was lying face down on the carpet in my piss-soaked underwear. Despite having been out of my skull on booze for the last three days—unreachable by phone, decency, or death—I'd still found the kind of strength only doting fathers can summon for their darling daughters; the strength to open the one eye that wasn't buried in the carpet and watch her little feet walk over to the front door. There, she'd paused by my soiled, urine- and booze-soaked clothes I'd dutifully left on the welcome mat of our family home for someone else to deal with. Then, I'd watched those little feet turn and approach the wreckage of her father, kneel, and lie next to me, her face just inches from mine.

"Why didn't my baby gorilla put me to bed last night like you promised?" she asked again.

I didn't have an answer for her—not a good enough one.

The thing was: the gorilla she wanted me to be—the strong, gentle, loyal, emotionally intelligent, one who swung from trees—was not the gorilla I believed I was or could ever become. I thought I was hard-wired as a different kind of gorilla: a wounded, broken one; misunderstood, vulnerable, emotionally isolated, and overdependent on a malignant inner tyrant. And this morning, I think Finley began to realize that.

She asked again, patiently giving me every opportunity to explain away the terrible reality that was dawning on her on this golden morning; a reality no child should ever have to confront.

I didn't say a word.

I *wanted* to.

I *wanted* to say, "I'm *sorry*," but I knew it would sound hollow. I'd said that too many times before in similar situations and countless other equally worthless variants. Yet here I was again. So, how sorry was I? Clearly not enough to change my behavior. So, I spared her the insult of a fake apology.

I *wanted* to say, "I *love* you," but I didn't want her to associate love with this version of me—or anyone else, for that matter. What comfort could that phrase give a child when paired with such neglect and abdication of responsibility? If my baby gorilla were to stand a chance in life, she shouldn't grow up with any ingrained belief that this conduct—how I had turned up, or *failed* to turn up for her—had anything to do with love. So, I spared her that insult, too.

There was so much I wanted to say, but anything I could have said would have been an insult to her, and I was so, *so* tired of doing that. So, instead, I just lay in silence, with a beet-red face, in my wet underwear, with tears running down my cheeks, looking into her eyes. That was my best option. That was the best I could do. And she lay there, in silence, in her pink princess jammies, her face just inches from mine, glowing in the golden morning light that reflected off the tears running down her cheeks, looking back into my eyes.

In a strong field, this moment has to be one of the most valued of my life; one I'd been waiting for—working tirelessly toward—for 23 years.

Finally, here it was. Job done. I had found what I was looking for.

So, why *didn't* Finley's baby gorilla tuck her in? And what justification could I possibly have for describing the above scene as anything other than a moral obscenity?

These questions are simple enough and the right ones to ask.

The answers, however, are more complex, but I'll give them my best shot, anyway, in the following pages.

It all started 23 years before, on a sunny evening in San Diego, in 1997.

blind landing

/ˈblaɪnd ˈlændɪŋ/ **noun**

*A dismount or tumbling pass completed without visual contact
with the floor. Requires muscle memory, trust, and full
commitment. Mistakes here are common, but almost always
part of the process.*

I want to get to that sunny San Diego evening in 1997 as soon
as possible. I want to get to *everything* as soon as possible.
That's the kind of person I am and have always been. That was
the kind of *kid* I was; the *speedy, hyper-energetic* kind. But, over
time, I've learned that context helps tell a story, so I'll blast
through a few establishing details that lead up to when my fuse
was lit.

    I was born in southern California in 1985 and grew up in
Jamul, a small, dusty town just outside San Diego, surrounded
by stretches of dry grass, pepper trees, hills, and dirt trails. It
was peaceful. So peaceful that if you weren't careful, you
might hear your own thoughts or the neighbors arguing.

What happens behind other people's doors has always intrigued me. Maybe it was because I wanted to understand their problems, but more likely, it was because I wanted reassurance that our house was normal, or that I was normal.

Dad was a preacher, Mom was a teacher, and I was the third of four kids. Our home was like the family version of the irresistible force meeting the immovable object. We kids had space, energy, ideas, and ambition—we were the irresistible force. And Mom and Dad combined were the immovable object, running the house with rules, structure, Bible studies, and prayers. I was raised on values and memory verses, with church deeply woven into our daily lives. I believe my parents loved us and gave everything they had to offer. Their way of showing love was through rules and expectations—to be good, obedient, strong, and a reflection of the faith in which they raised us.

That's what I wanted to be: good, obedient, and strong.

However, I was gifted (if that's the right word) with a particularly, umm... manic energy. Fortunately, the hills served as my playground. I didn't care much for silence, reflection, or stillness. When I drank from the cup of life, it was in the same way a marathon runner passing the 20-mile water station might; I grabbed it, spilled it, splashed it on my face, tossed the cup aside, and kept going. I was always running, riding, climbing, building, and flipping. I craved motion like other kids craved candy. But my motion was unrefined, and I struggled to fit in.

My other siblings seemed to have everything figured out: "L" was the college-bound athlete with self-control as strong as his shoulders. "C" was also athletic but could zone in—or out, depending on your perspective—and lose himself in video games. And then there was little "M"—or should that be written, "m." She was a bird whisperer who brought light and softness to the house by raising baby geese and chickens. Each of my siblings had their talents on which they focused. In comparison, I was the loon who came home bruised, cut, scraped, dirty, and amped after having burned off some—but never all—of that day's excess energy; coming home to the silence, the rules, the demands to sit still, and the prayers before dinner.

Like I said: Unstoppable Force, meet Immovable Object.

(I sometimes felt like a caged gorilla. I've already mentioned that I like gorillas. I relate to them. They've become a recurring theme for me. At their best, they are strong, gentle, loyal, and they swing from trees. What's not to love? But they can also be misunderstood, vulnerable, and slow to adapt. Worse, they tend to withdraw into isolation when wounded. They can also be overly dependent on a dominant leader, even if that leader is harmful, even if that harmful leader is internal. The similarity between this duality and my own struggles is not lost on me.)

The rules of the family home didn't accommodate my physicality, and Mom and Dad didn't understand that there might be more going on in me than just excess energy, so, yeah, home was tough. And not just at home; school, too, was a disaster—another kind of cage. The law of this jungle was survival of the nerdiest, the quietest, or, perhaps most critically, the survival of those who could *sit still* and retain information. I could do none of the above, to an impressive degree.

There might be diagnoses today for which I could have been a poster child—conditions with pharmaceutical and therapeutic treatments that would turn the feral into the compliant. But back then—the late 80s and early 90s—no such diagnoses existed, and I was no poster child; I didn't suffer *from* a problem—I *was* the problem: I was the "instigator," the "disruption," the "clown," the "failure." I was the one who got caught sneaking out and lighting something on fire just to see what would happen. I loved to pester people just to get a reaction. I was the "Pester" child.

My parents and teachers tried everything—from flashcards and reading drills to positive encouragement to various threats and disciplinary actions—to get me to sit still and succeed in the way *they* defined success, but nothing worked.

Worse than this failure to meet *external* definitions of success was my failure to meet *internal* ones. The harder they tried to help me, the more I saw the light and hope in their eyes slowly fade, no doubt caused by worry, exhaustion, and the heartbreak that any parent would feel when loving a kid they can't reach. And as their hope for me faded, so did *my* hope for me.

Was I broken? I began to believe I was.

So, what the hell was going on?

* * *

I loved my family. I still do, and I know they loved me. But love doesn't always equate to understanding. Sometimes, the safest places are also where we first learn how to hide, and I learned early how to hide extremely well. Humor, mischief, and defiance were my first-generation masks. And beneath that mask, I carried a weight for which I didn't have words, like pent-up potential energy, and this energy manifested in many ways.

Physically, I had energy for days, but with nowhere to put it—never enough time to burn it. My brain was fast, my body faster, and school felt like a prison of mind, body, and spirit. In relatable terms, I was that kid who wore down his shoes faster than anyone else. I ground my teeth, and I constantly fidgeted.

And it wasn't just hyperactivity; there was anxiety tucked in there, too. A buzzing under my skin that never switched off, as if 20 people were talking to me all at once. I was also unusually sensitive. Rejection, embarrassment, and disapproval didn't just sting; they gutted me. While sensitivity would eventually become something I realized could also be a strength, as a kid, unable to process it properly, it made me vulnerable. I found myself perpetually bracing for something. I couldn't name it, but I felt it, and I needed to be ready for it, braced for impact.

Not even in sleep could I find peace. I was frequently woken by night terrors. This restlessness—this "dis-ease" in me—was being driven by something complex, lurking deep down.

As a child, I couldn't express any of this verbally. And when it expressed itself, be it physically or emotionally, at home or school, that didn't work either. It was an intense and constant itch to *do something*—impossible to ignore, and I was disciplined when I didn't repress it. The older I got, the more intense it became and the harder I had to work to contain the compulsion to move. All the while, my family and teachers grew increasingly exasperated with me, and the pressure, fear, and anxiety within me—to not be bad by moving too much—kept building. Each time I slipped up, it triggered greater repercussions, frustrations, disappointment, and disciplinary action, and a spiraling decline in my self-worth.

It was as if I were a grenade with the pin pulled out, trying not to explode. I was a nervous wreck.

This grenade inside me caused restlessness, fractured home life, chaotic school years, shame, and a feeling of inadequacy. I wrestled with it relentlessly, determined to stop it. And when I first started gymnastics, I found a way to channel my energy.

The gym was the only place where I felt truly myself, truly at home. Gymnastics gave me something the rest of life could not: structure *and* freedom, at the *same time*. I started at a place called Aztec Gymnastics and trained from the age of eight to twelve under a guy named Ben Miller. Ben then introduced me to Steve Butcher, an Olympic coach and judge, and one of the most charismatic people I have ever met.

If there's one person I can point to as a steady compass in the early chaos of my life, it's Steve Butcher. Long before I had any confidence in myself, he saw something in me—some flicker of curiosity or drive—and chose to nurture it. He was my coach, but also more than that: a father figure, a mentor, a refuge. The gym was the first place I felt safe being myself, and Steve created space for that. He never pushed with force; he inspired with presence. I wasn't the best in my age group, but he made me feel like I belonged anyway. He taught me how to be focused, how to take feedback, and how to care about the details. Looking back, the discipline and grit I strive to bring to my life today—especially in my relationships with my kids, my work, and my recovery—started with him. He didn't just coach gymnastics. He coached character and led with heart. Many of the qualities he displayed sowed seeds in me for what I wanted to become as a father and a business leader. I didn't know that at the time, of course, but I felt it.

When I met Steve, a light bulb lit up. If he had walked over to me and said, *"Hi, young Daniel, I'm grown-up Daniel—I'm a coach, mentor, father, and awesome guy—I'm the version of you that you will aspire to be for the rest of your life,"* it would not have been any clearer to me that he had what I wanted. More accurately and importantly, he had what I knew I had the potential to become. He had a significant impact on me. Steve Butcher wore a T-shirt with flashing neon lettering that read, *"I'm your future—brace for impact."*

It was an interesting time. Steve wasn't the only person who impressed me so profoundly.

Melanie was my childhood friend, the kind who knew our house, my family, and my quirks. We grew up in the same world—bare feet on trampolines, chalk dust in the air, and long summer days that seemed to stretch forever. She was the kind of girl who didn't need to talk to make you feel good. I don't know why I say she was "the kind of girl," though, because she was one of a kind. She was quiet, steady, and observant, just like I was a storm in a T-shirt—loud, funny, and unpredictable. Yet somehow, we understood each other. She understood me when no one else did. She wore the same T-shirt, the one that said, *"I'm your future—brace for impact."* It looked good on her.

If only I'd paid more attention to that.

If only.

There was one other place I'd seen those words. I'd also seen them in a garbage bag during the summer of 1997. I was 12. The flashing neon lettering was buzzing, starting quietly, then growing louder, drawing my attention. But this buzzing, flickering neon lettering crackled in a different way. The allure was the same, but that crackling—that arcing—hinted at faulty wiring, dangerous electric undercurrents, and shocks.

If only I'd paid more attention to them.

If only.

My dad had just turned 50, and he'd thrown a big party—big by our standards, at least. We were a close-knit church family, with structure and rules, but this was his 50th birthday—a significant milestone that deserved a proper celebration on our two-acre property. There were family, friends, music, food, and plenty of alcohol. I didn't drink. Drinking was against the rules.

When it was over, they didn't clean everything up right away. For over a week, a few 50-gallon trash cans sat near the barn, filled with melted ice, floating cans, and leftover beer. Most of it was Bud and Coors Light. I remember seeing the red, white, and gold cans catch the light, glinting like hidden treasure (and crackling with hidden menace).

I could see them from the backyard trampoline. Day after day, as I tried to bounce the energy out, I'd see them. I heard those neon letters buzzing—*I'm your future*—and watched those cans catch the light. I don't know if it was the freedom they represented, curiosity, or the lure of something forbidden and against the rules—most likely a cocktail of the lot. Whatever it was, I eventually stopped jumping on the trampoline, looked around to make sure no one was watching, climbed down, walked over to the garbage bag, and picked up a can.

It was lukewarm and slippery. I cracked it open and took a sip. It was flat, bitter, and perfect, and I sat with that beer for about an hour, sipping and feeding my curiosity drop by drop. After that, everything felt just a little bit funnier, just a little lighter. It was as if the pressure within me was being released, one sip at a time, as if someone had replaced the pin back into the grenade. I could breathe. I felt in control; more able to be good.

The taste didn't matter; what mattered was how it made me feel: just a little bit more normal, just a little bit less broken. I just wanted to be a good boy. I didn't want to be the crazy kid who always got in trouble. And this drink seemed to lower the pressure.

All the next day at school, all I thought about was how beer made me feel. And after school, I returned to the garbage bag, where I sat and drip-fed my soul.

And I did the same the next day.

And the next.

No one noticed the cans disappearing; there were so many to begin with, I wasn't making a dent. I started timing my chores and homework around sneaking a beer, and afterward, I'd run around the property with a buzz that felt like electricity in my limbs, and a confidence that made me feel like I wasn't a bad kid.

I didn't get "drunk" in any way that was visible or do anything wild. I didn't get caught. I didn't get sick. This was just a 12-year-old kid with a can of Coors Light. I did, however, find something that made me feel better in my own skin.

I drank to tame the wounded gorilla in me.

I drank to put the pin back into the grenade.

I drank to believe that everything was going to be ok.

It was a warm, sunny evening in San Diego in 1997. I was 12 years old. I pulled a lukewarm, slippery can of beer out of the garbage bag, sat down, cracked it open, and read the neon lettering on its side that glistened gold in the setting sun. *"I'm your future. Brace for impact."*

And I drank to my future, but I did not brace for its impact.

That was the day Death got the memo. That was the day he started looking for me.

And the thing about Death is, he's a cunning little bastard. And he's patient—so patient. Death has all the time in the world for those whose days are numbered. And that day, Death got my number.

The other thing about Death is that he doesn't care for conquests, per se. No. Death revels more in the pursuit—the *chase*—like a cat toys with a mouse. It is the flirting with Death that is the more terrible dance, the near-Death experience, the crueler torment. For this is the dance that ruins not one soul but many, and not just once but many times, again and again, until one way or another, the music finally stops, and the dance is finally over.

whipback

/ˈwɪpˌbæk/ *noun*

A fast, snapping back handspring with no pause or setup. Velocity created by momentum alone. Often appears when the body is reacting faster than the mind.

It started like a whisper, something to take the edge off, numb the anxiety, release the pressure, heal the damaged neurology, or whatever the problem was. But it didn't stay a whisper for long—not for me, at least. For me, back then, it soon made a compelling case that I was a better person when I partnered with it. Once I felt the evidence, believed it, and was swayed by its case, I was hooked and compelled to view alcohol as my ticket to being the best version of myself.

But the compulsion was deceitful: as I followed it, the prize it offered seemed ever elusive—never satisfying. And like a naïve fucking idiot, I followed it down one dark turn after another, deeper and deeper into a labyrinth, without any clue I was being set up.

It would be years before things got dark, years before the ER visits, the blackouts, and the shame became the norm. But when I look back, I can draw a straight line from that moment in 1997, when I grabbed a beer out of a garbage can, to when I staggered into an LA emergency room, where machines saved my life.

People often think that the life of an alcoholic starts with chaos already as its seed, a nihilistic drive. Not for me, it didn't. For me, it began with a slow drip of quiet moments—the first raindrops on a mirror-smooth pond; one beer at a time, one escape at a time—that gradually grew in scope, number, and intensity, until those ripples merged and distorted my reflection, rendering it unrecognizable.

By the time I reached adolescence, just a year or two after my first beer, I was hooked on the stuff, the feeling, and the ruse. I wasn't just drinking booze; I was using it. I wasn't just acting out, I was unraveling. Yet I remained convinced I was pursuing the best version of me. I wanted success—as a family man, and a businessman—and saw that future reflected in drink. But that image was a mirage.

I still managed to fool most people, of course. I was quick-witted, athletic, and could make people laugh. I still didn't have a name for my problem, nor for what felt like the solution. But drinking had a way of making me feel larger, funnier, quicker, more daring in my athleticism; a better version of me. It also emboldened my denial that drinking had anything to do with that better me.

And all the while, behind the mask of extraversion lay a void in me that I was ignoring. I became inflated with a bravado that distracted me from the very scrutiny and honest introspection that might well have helped me fill it with the good stuff: life lessons, wisdom, and maturity. But I was too busy looking out for my vulnerabilities to look in at them or, better yet, to look *after* them. As my peer group matured, my inner, wounded gorilla lay in a dark hole, stunted and starved... I guess.

Because who knows?

All I know is that, over the next few years—throughout my early teens—I drank more and more, pursuing the mirage of my desired future. And more and more, I feared being alone with my sober mind and the thoughts of failure, emptiness, boredom, mundanity, and mediocrity that languished. As time went on, I found my trajectory accelerating, chasing the esteem I *wanted* while running from the esteem I *lacked*.

Over the course of a year or two—the timelines are unclear, still—I initially fueled this endeavor with more beer, and then with liquor. And when drunk, I stoked it further through attention-seeking stunts, daring performances, and anything else that would sate this now demanding addiction that was starting to feel more like a runaway train. Still, I was now committed to the ruse—I needed to maintain the facade I'd established—so I stoked it; upping my dose, upping my game, upping my needs.

And while I still hadn't attached a label to my delusion (or if I had, it wasn't one I was willing to accept and so quickly buried), its name was not far from the surface. This was not the first such runaway train I'd seen. Runaway trains ran in the family.

My grandmother died in her early 40s. She struggled with addiction to stimulants and alcohol during a time when mental illness wasn't talked about, and institutionalization was the societal solution. She was in and out of facilities whose staff didn't understand the problem or receive the necessary training to offer the appropriate guidance—either to her or the rest of the family—and left behind a trail of pain, confusion, shame, and stoic silence, which only deepened the family's dysfunction.

My parents never spoke about it, except for the rare times they caught fleeting glimpses of her in me, a dubious honor.

"You remind me of your Grandmother," I was told on more than one occasion. "Her energy, her charisma, her pain."

"Her fate, too?" I wondered to myself.

This mirage had made many promises over generations to many in my family. Addiction was her name. Her snake oil came in many vials, colors, and varieties; alcoholism was just one of her treatments, workaholism another, and there was perfectionism, rage, emotional withdrawal, gambling—and the list goes on—hollow promises masking contracts with the devil. Addiction ran in the family; she was an unspoken, invisible, perpetual guest in our home, and it seemed that we made her feel very welcome. We were gracious hosts, whether we knew it or not.

* * *

It was not only my grandmother's energy, charisma, and pain that my mother saw in me.

"You have her gift," was another likeness she saw, referring to our innate knack with kids.

Even when I was young, I didn't just *play with* other kids; I *entertained* them and took charge. I'd chase them, scare them, dare them, and laugh with them. And I didn't do it just for a few minutes. I could do it for hours. I could do it all day. I'd say I was the ringleader, but that term has negative connotations, and early on, my "leadership" wasn't negative. Later, in my late teens and twenties, it was—100%—but as a kid, my games were creative, fun, and engaging in the best ways.

Because of my dad's work, we spent a lot of time at church. He ran Sunday School, and the church offered childcare during services, so I couldn't help but volunteer with the children's ministry, assist in the daycare, rock babies, and play with toddlers. It was where I wanted to be, and they were who I wanted to be with. There was something about babies in those tiny fleece onesies, tucked in like beetles, hands curled under their cheeks, sucking their fingers in their sleep, that made me melt and draw me in. I'd picture putting my own kid in a front pack, walking around with them strapped to my chest, taking them everywhere I went. Even at the age of ten, I recall knowing that I loved working with kids, inspiring them, and that I wanted to have my own.

Perhaps it was because I was still a kid inside, or that I found the adult world so unwelcoming and even hostile to my true nature. I often felt like I didn't fit in with adults. I always felt at home with kids. They are honest, raw, and fun. They don't expect you to have your life together; they just want to play. I couldn't meet the constantly rising bar of expectations set by my parents and school, and by age 12, I'd found a way to cope with that. But what I *could* do—very well, as it turned out—was lead kids and teach them how to burn off their own energy.

At church events, birthday parties, or family gatherings, whenever kids were around, they'd follow me. If I climbed a tree, other kids would follow. If I did flips or handstands, other kids would follow. They knew I'd chase them, joke with them, make them laugh, and most importantly, they knew I'd pay attention to them. I wasn't an adult telling them to calm down; I was the one encouraging them to be more energetic. I was the one mentoring them, caring for them. I was the one bringing out the best in them. I was coaching them. After meeting Ben at Aztec, he recognized this in me and offered me a part-time job, which I jumped at.

It wasn't a glamorous job, but it was honest: teaching weekend gymnastics classes at Aztec, a little program that ran alongside the San Diego State University gymnastics team. Every Saturday and Sunday for the next four years, I showed up to teach and used the money to gain more independence, like getting my own cell phone and later paying for gas and car insurance. The job taught me responsibility and leadership, even if I was only guiding a class of six-year-olds in cartwheels and handstands. And it gave me purpose, confidence, and independence.

This opportunity wasn't a big leap; it was simply a continuation of what I've always done and been. Teaching came naturally. I loved helping kids try new things, watching their confidence grow, and knowing I played a part in that. If the deep reward I sought was connection, coaching gymnastics, I soon realized, was the perfect way for me to achieve that while staying true to myself.

I became a bit of a duality: While one side of me struggled to fit into adult life and drank more and more to cope with what was missing, the other half thrived by coaching gymnastics and mentoring kids. And, for a moment, I found some balance—a fragile truce. It was not an easy ceasefire, mind you; both sides were highly charged. It was more like a well-matched tug of war, static but loaded, with the rope beginning to fray.

And after the Maxima incident, it snapped.

* * *

By the time I was 16, I still didn't know what my dark side was; I hadn't yet labeled it. I still felt that there was some control in my life, solid ground beneath my feet, and security, as if this world was one big trampoline. I was doing well at Aztec, managing in school, and I'd secured a second part-time job at a local video store. (My addiction demanded good cash flow.) I was driving, and things were okay. Every time I fell, the safety net was there to catch me. And my mom's Nissan Maxima was working fine. But this fragile truce was about to collapse.

I'd just finished a late shift at Hollywood Video in Lemon Grove. It was around midnight, and the parking lot was mostly empty and poorly lit. Exhausted after putting away hundreds of DVDs and cassettes, I was ready to get home and had cash in my pocket. I walked out to the Maxima, opened the door, and sat down in the driver's seat.

Before I even shut the door, some crack-head rushed the car, slid into the passenger seat, and was already waiting for me. He was huge: a six-foot-five guy, tweaker thin but big-boned and intimidating, and fast... and *quiet*. By the time I turned to see what was going on, there he was.

I hadn't invited him. I didn't know him. He was just there: a six-foot-five, 250 lb threat, dressed in jeans and an ironic t-shirt, with a box of menthol cigarettes, sat in the passenger seat, making the decisions. What a metaphor for my life.

"Drive," he said in a quiet, deep, controlled voice.

I considered asserting some kind of dominance, but this guy was seasoned. It was bad enough that he was big and intimidating. But worse, he was calm, as if this was his daily routine; calm in the way dangerous people are. An insecure threat would have argued with me, or raised his voice; a secure one wouldn't care about me. And he didn't care. This interaction was not a negotiation; it was a *monologue*, a series of *instructions*; a *one-man show* in which I was merely a prop, a mode of transport, a ticket to be used and discarded.

"Drive," he repeated, in that same calm, controlled tone.

And so, I drove.

I didn't ask where or why. Nor did I ask what he was hiding under his ironic T-shirt. It could have been a gun, a knife, or a sandwich. And I wondered what else was going to appear in this lurid scene. I tried to read his ironic T-shirt, but thought better of it, uncertain what I would do with whatever information I discovered. I even remember running through the scenarios.

"What if it's a cool T?" I thought as my inner monologue ran wild. "Should I *say* something? Is that appropriate in a carjacking? What about something like *'Yeah, Heisenberg! Science, Mr. White,'* to try to connect with him? Or maybe, *'Plans for the Death Star? Nice. Personally, I'm an OG Episode 4 guy.'* Oh, god, don't use OG. What if it's less nerdy, somehow more threatening, whatever that might be? [Insert worst-case scenario.] Is seeing that going to do me any favours? Why am I even *thinking* these things?"

Maybe this guy was just down on his luck, looking for a ride, some cash, or even just some company. Or maybe I'd be dead before dawn, stuffed in some dumpster or ditch to be found days later by a runner, a dog walker, or a garbage collector.

My heart was pounding, but I held it together and drove wherever he wanted, left then right, left then right. As I did, my thoughts took similar turns, shifting from his T to who I'd prefer to find my body: the runner, the dog walker, or the garbage collector. There was something romantic, almost poetic, about being discovered by the garbage guy. The runner and the dog-walker seemed too mundane, and I wasn't interested in the mundane; that, somehow, wasn't me.

It was a twisted inner monologue. The truth was that I was stuck in a moment that didn't seem real. In any life-threatening situation, crisis, or drama, life goes on until it doesn't. And while it does, the busy brain can complain or be in panic mode for only so long. I bet, when the Titanic went down, after all the drama had settled and reality sank in, some people in the life rafts started thinking, "I wonder if this qualifies me for a refund," or "How are we supposed to go to the bathroom?"

Looking back, I think I was too young and naïve to realize the gravity of the situation or the danger I was in. I didn't take it seriously. After all, life was like a trampoline, was it not? But in that moment, I wasn't looking back; I was looking *forward*, and my mind was consumed with what was written on the guy's T-shirt, what he was hiding *under* it, and that I was kind of low on gas.

He directed me through Lemon Grove, eventually turning into a trash- and dumpster-filled alley where another silhouetted, shadowy figure was waiting; this one a weathered, skinny, older white guy.

That's where I started to get the chills. At this point, the dumpster end-game seemed less poetic after all, and the runner and dog walker began to feel like better options. I started to not like the idea of dying. I started to want to delay that outcome.

"Pull over," said the guy.

I pulled over.

"Keys," he said, holding out his hand.

I gave him my keys.

"Wallet," he said.

I complied.

He got out of the car and approached the skinny white guy. They talked for a few moments, occasionally looking over in my direction. Then they both walked back toward me and got in the car. By now, I wasn't interested in his T-shirt. I wanted to be home.

Once the doors were closed, they pulled out a glass pipe and started smoking what I assumed was crack cocaine, passing it between them in silence; getting their hit, getting their relief, releasing their own inner pressure.

I sat motionless as the car filled with a thick, chemical fume that reeked of burnt plastic and anguish. I watched this sinister and cynical smoke curl through the air. The shit I'd become addicted to—beer and hard liquor—seemed so clean and innocent compared to the dark, bleak, sad, seedy chemical fix these guys needed. And the irony that it was all playing out in my mom's Nissan Maxima seemed to make a mockery of the moment. If I had seen this in a movie, it would not have been in a Nissan unless it was a spoof. It was a tense cinematic moment playing out in the banality of my mom's car.

After they got high, a new, unpredictable threat began to permeate the air. That was the moment when my fear for my life leveled up. I started to shake.

"Drive," he said again as he handed back my keys and empty wallet—still calm, but now changed; darker. If there was any part of me that related to the version of him when he first got into my car—and that's a *big if*—this altered, corrupted version of him, by contrast, was something altogether alien; something I didn't know and couldn't read, much less predict or reason with.

The car was out of gas, so, after getting his permission, I pulled into the nearest station. When I turned off the car, the two men exited for a smoke, and that's when another guy yelled from across the parking lot.

"Hey! Muthafuckas," he yelled. "What you doing in the white kid's car? Get the fuck outta there!"

And as quickly as the incident had started, it was over.

The smoke in the car cleared in no time. The smell lingered for days. But the feeling stayed with me for the rest of my life; not fear, per se, but a sense of existential insecurity— a loss of innocence.

The Nissan Maxima incident marked a turning point; the moment I realized the world was not a trampoline, when the veil of civility was lifted, revealing how fragile we are and how close danger lurks when we're not paying attention.

That was my first real encounter with hard drugs, my first glimpse into a lost world—one in which I would soon be immersed. It wasn't a friendly introduction, but then again, how could it be? What would be the polite etiquette for such an introduction? It seemed in hindsight to be perfectly choreographed, perfectly pitched.

I had been hijacked, robbed, and subjected to fear and darkness. Framed this way, the introduction was fitting.

Part of me broke loose that night. I felt a new itch. I saw the next level of this game I was in. I no longer felt secure. This was no longer a kid's game; shit just got real. This was serious, threatening, seedy, and... dare I say, interesting.

I hadn't realized there were more levels in this existential labyrinth, more sub-basements to explore, more steps to descend as I followed my path downward, not until that night. But after the Maxima incident, I knew. And once a self-destructive psyche realizes there's a next level, it kind of gets curious.

That was it: that was what was written on that guy's T-shirt.

"I'm your future; Brace for impact."

parallel bars

/ˈpærəˌlɛl bɑːrz/ *noun*

Two evenly spaced bars used in a routine requiring continuous motion and control. Balance, tension, and alignment are key. The space between is just as important as the grip on each side.

Some days in our lives stand out as key turning points. Usually, these days are not ones we could have predicted or planned in advance. Most of the time, they remain unknown to us even as we wake up on those fateful days. Sometimes, they stay a mystery even after the day is over. In these moments—such as the day I met Liz and Rob, or Melanie, or, more tangentially, pre-destined and fatalistic, when I met the people who would *introduce* me to them—the importance of the day only becomes clear over time. Only then can we look back and think, "My God, what if I hadn't met them that day, or gone this way instead of that? How would my life have turned out?" These are tiny events during which we unknowingly step into some alternate future (or not), and after that, everything changes.

The moments when, for example, we meet our future spouse, mentor, or best friend for life—every relationship-based event—tend to be uneventful at the time because, by their nature, they are relationship-based; on day one, the relationship hasn't yet developed.

That summer evening in 1997 was a big day for me, but only in retrospect.

The day I met Melanie, Liz, and Rob; the same.

The day I walked into Gyminny Kids; the same.

The day I met Steve Butcher was a bit different. He made an immediate impression on me.

But June 13, 2003? That was a day I recognized as important in real time, for four distinct reasons.

One: I graduated from high school.

That was a big deal, not because I graduated. And what does that word even mean? When everyone who hasn't been expelled shows up for graduation, the standards are pretty low. I gave my school plenty of reasons to fail me, but despite much hand-wringing, I couldn't even convince them I didn't deserve rejection. And so, I graduated. Yay for me, and for the resentment I built up while I was in that cage. After June 13, 2003, I'd never be subject to school rules again.

Two: I turned 18.

Legally, I was now an adult, responsible for my own decisions. While this shifted much of the responsibility from my parents to me—something an irresponsible kid might shy away from—this was precisely why it mattered to me. After June 13, 2003, I'd never be subject to parental rules again.

Three: I moved out of my parents' house and into my own digs.

They might have been shitty digs—scratch that: they *were* shitty digs—but they were *mine*. My digs, my front door. My keys. My rules. And so, my life on my schedule began. After June 13, 2003, I'd never again be subject to my parents' house rules.

And four: I pulled into a car wash.

This was tangential, predestined, and fatalistic, triggering a series of events that would define the rest of my life—and arguably, the lives of thousands of others.

* * *

After the Nissan Maxima carjacking, I found myself teetering on the edge. Let me rephrase that: A better analogy might be that I found myself "almost derailing."

Derailing is a phrase that has its standard implication of being diverted from one's course. I had stood at a black doorway that led to the lower levels of self-destruction. But I was not ready for that descent—not yet. I did not derail. But I thought about it.

And derailing has other useful connotations I can use. Rail tracks are parallel, and up until the carjacking, my life was neatly divided into two parallel lives. There was the clean life (school, home, and the gym) and the party life (bars, parties, and booze). They ran parallel: They never crossed (if I could help it), and, for a while, I lived separate but parallel lives.

But after the carjacking, it was as if that was no longer the case: Sometimes, they would diverge and become impossible to reconcile, pushing me to my limits and occasionally forcing me to choose one over the other. That was painful and, at times, messy. At other times, these paths would cross, and that was even worse. Whether I brought my now chaotic habit into the family home or didn't go home at all and made my legally responsible parents find me, the house of rules was invaded by unwelcome truths. I'd become a problem, and now, everyone knew it.

Something had to give, and eventually, something did, on June 13, 2003.

But while "my life on my schedule" sounded nice, the subtext was, "my bar bills and my need to pay for them."

I needed a job.

The only thing I was ever any good at was gym, and on that same day, June 13, I recalled my first interactions with Steve Butcher. I'd always loved the gym. I'd made it my home. My coaches had become my surrogate family, and I aspired to become what they were to me: a mentor, a coach, someone to admire, someone to learn from, a father figure.

In my experience, parenting and coaching share many similarities. I didn't *want* them to be similar, but in my experience, they *were*. What *I* wanted was for the roles to be discrete, parallel, and complementary, and the more I thought about coaching, the more I differentiated it from parenting.

In the vision I had for my future self, I saw the role of the coach as providing the technical guidance needed to win, the work ethic required to excel, and the structure to develop a successful athlete. He might yell at us, but that was okay. His job is not to love us or hug us; it is to train the athlete to win. On the other hand, a parent's role is to love us and hug us, regardless of where we finish. If my upbringing and my role in it blurred that distinction, there was little I could do about it now. However, as I started to consider becoming a coach, this division of labor became very clear to me. I wanted to be both a coach to gym kids—pushing them to become physically strong—and a father—hugging my own kids regardless of external metrics of success, offering them a safe space to grow emotionally confident. *That's* what I wanted. *That* was my goal.

I might have been a fuck-up. Scratch that; I *was* a fuck up. But even fuck-ups can know what they want. We don't *choose* to be a fuck up. More often, we are a fuck-up precisely because we lack the skills needed to become what we aspire to be. Or, more nuanced, because we invest in the wrong things to get us to where we want to be. Fuck-up or not, I aspired to be an encouraging coach and a loving dad.

The dad thing; that felt far off. By the age of 18, Melanie—my barefoot trampoline friend—and I had dated on and off. It was a work in progress. I was emotionally stuck, with the maturity of a 12-year-old and driven by the hormones of a hyperactive, alcoholic 18-year-old. We still had that deep understanding we'd always shared, which is great in the spiritual world, but in the material world, I was a jackass. So, yeah, like I said, the Dad thing felt far off.

And as for the coaching? The Aztec thing had run its course, and I needed a new job. As I drove around looking for a carwash, I reflected on what to do next.

* * *

Many people see gymnastics as beautiful, graceful, and polished. That's the goal: to make it *appear* like that. But as anyone who has ever trained to refine any activity can attest, it's not the reality.

When we watch someone on, say, the parallel bars, we see the rewards of a thousand falls. We don't see the parallel universe that got them there, nor the pain that is as much a part of a gymnast's life as their breakfast. We applaud the heights of their achievement but are spared the rope burns suffered in their ascent. We seek the bright eyes and glowing skin of health, but are shielded from shin bruises so deep they turn black, yellow, and green all at once. We see their sturdy two-foot landings, but not the endless repetitions demanded by their ambition that push them until either their muscles or their stomachs give out. It's not just a sport; it's a baptism by repetition.

And for me, that baptism gave me not just relief from my inner turmoil but also control over it. In my distorted view of the world, any pain I went through during training was a full-frontal assault on *its attack* on my self-worth. I wasn't just trying to sweat out the devil inside me; I was trying to beat the shit out of it, and I constantly earned wounds and rewards from my efforts.

I was competing seriously and training like a man possessed. I would spend hours doing circles on the pommel horse until my hands blistered. My legs would bang against the wood countless times until my shins swelled or even split open. Training hurt like hell—and it quieted the turmoil; my mind would fade for a little while in the intensity of the moment.

The more it hurt, the more I felt like I was normal. Pain was a balm.

Flexibility drills were a special kind of balm. Coaches would push me into splits, press down on my back, and I would grit my teeth through the burn. Most kids dreaded those days, but I needed them. Physical pain made emotional pain easier to bear. It was a form of exorcism, self-medication, a ritualistic effort to purge.

I didn't have emotional tools for managing my fear, sadness, or anxiety, and I'd do anything that would give me a sense of control. The first place I found that control was through gymnastics. In the gym, I could build my body into something strong, worthy, and noteworthy—something people clapped for. I learned how to get back up and do hard things again and again, even when I didn't want to. Ultimately, gymnastics taught me that progress was possible. Repetition always makes progress possible.

Gymnastics couldn't fix what was happening inside, but I could stick the landing. It didn't save me, but it bought me time and taught me the real lessons I needed so that, when the moment came for me to save myself, I knew that transformation was possible.

Those lessons, as it turned out, would become invaluable later when I had to rebuild my life, my family, and my business. I had no idea of that at the time, and I wonder what would have become of me had I not found the gym. But that's another universe.

Where was I? Oh, yeah: June 13, 2003.

* * *

On June 13, the fourth significant event of the day was pulling into a car wash that, as it turned out, was owned by a friend's parents.

At the carwash, I asked for a job.

On the job, I met a guy who, a few weeks later, threw a house party.

At the house party, I met Elsworth and Gary and struck up a conversation with them.

During the conversation, we learned that we all loved gymnastics, they worked at Gymminy Kids (a gym I'd never heard of), I was looking for work, and that Gymminy Kids had opportunities.

"Dude, you should apply," said Gary. Four simple words, but so profound.

In life, if we ever find ourselves in a situation that fills us with doubt, we should just tell ourselves, "Dude, you should apply." Because, whatever the outcome, we'll never know who we might meet, and if we don't apply, we never will.

So, I applied for work at Gyminny Kids, and that's when I met Liz and Rob:

Liz and Rob; remember the names.

Liz was the captain of the ship, making business decisions with a mix of sharp business acumen and a matriarchal heart. When I met her, I was still 18, muscular, tan, and a bit cocky. I had been lifting heavy for two years straight, could bench 315 pounds for reps, and could crank out over 40 strict pull-ups without breaking a sweat. I looked the part of a men's gymnast, exuded the confidence of a coach, and had entrepreneurial energy, all of which caught Liz's attention.

Rob was Liz's husband. He was more like a playful grandpa. He taught preschool classes and brought a warm, goofy energy to the gym. He wore bright colors, made silly noises, and connected with little kids in a way I admired, related to, and could naturally imitate. He wasn't just a coach; he was like magic to toddlers. I knew I could do that.

Between them, Liz and Rob had built Gyminny Kids, a wholesome and vibrant celebration of youthful energy, full of kids swinging and jumping, burning off all kinds of energy. And while they didn't have kids of their own, the Gyminny-Kids kids *were* their kids; this place was their family. And better still, everyone knew it. This place was a beloved home to thousands. It had discipline, structure, the gym, of course, love, mentorship, a warm feeling of home, parental guidance, and physical expression. There was the fun grandpa and the firm-but-fair mother figure.

Never before had I seen a place that had everything I wanted; it was also a place where I felt I could offer the most in return. In an adult world that seemed to reject me at every turn, this place seemed to celebrate and require the qualities I possessed, and the potential for exorcising the "qualities" that possessed me. Never before had I seen in my life a place that checked all of the healthy boxes on my list. Never before had I, in one snapshot, seen a place that felt so much like the home I one day wanted to create.

And if I felt like a poster child for Gyminny Kids, Liz saw it, too.

Men's gymnastics has always faced a bit of a stigma; it's not typically regarded as the most masculine of sports. So, when I walked into the gym with thick dark hair, strong arms, a bodybuilder's presence, and a deep love for kids, I believe Liz saw an opportunity. She sat me down, outlined her expectations, and hired me.

That car wash on June 13, 2003, was like a portal into a parallel universe. Had I not taken that turn, I never would have met the guy who introduced me to Gary. (Sorry, dude, I forgot your name, but thank you.) And I never would have met Liz and Rob, and I never would have become a coach at Gyminny Kids, the eight-figure gym brand I now own and run.

Had I turned into some other carwash, I might have driven myself, and maybe others, into a dumpster, to be found years later by a garbage collector, or worse, a runner or a dog walker, still holding a bottle of Johnny Walker in one hand and a running list of resentments in the other.

Even after my introduction to Gyminny Kids, I still did my best to find that dumpster, and there were many times over the next decade when I nearly reached that dark goal for myself, my family, and my kids.

For a moment—a brief moment—under the bright fluorescent lights hanging from the gym ceiling and the brighter glints in the eyes and smiles of everyone in the Gyminny family—my addiction would need another plan if it wanted to lure me into its shadows.

And that's precisely what it did: it stood back and came up with another plan.

pommel spiral

/ˈpɒməl ˈspaɪrəl/ **noun**

A circular swing motion executed on the pommel horse.
Requires rhythm over power. Loses form quickly if forced.

I was riding high: I had my own place, made my own rules, was still dating Melanie, and had a job where I felt appreciated for my talents. I was now 19, soon to be 20. Yeah, I was riding high.

The irony of insecurity, however, is that we—and when I say "we," I can only speak for myself, and even then, I was no more than a witness or co-conspirator at best; I was hardly an authority—seek ways to soothe that feeling of scarcity within. We want to feel good, so we cling to things—chase after things—that scratch our itch for validation and celebrate with disproportionate, and even inappropriate, zeal when we find even the most temporary relief.

I remember the first time I watched *Papillon*, starring Steve McQueen. The scene that stays with me is the one in which McQueen's character is in solitary confinement for a total of seven years, much of it spent in darkness and on half rations. As a result of such deprivation, even insects became treasured finds, eagerly devoured. I was disgusted the first time I saw the film, wondering how he could have endured such conditions. But when we are starved for nourishment, we become desperate, and those offerings jump to the top of the menu. To the thirsty, a gallon of dirty water will trump a sip of the pure stuff.

And so it was with me, too. I found relief in my superficial displays of success. I had a place to live, a way to cover the bills, a means to buy more expensive booze (and, by now, cocaine—as if I didn't already have enough energy), a personality that could entertain, and an insatiable need to outshine, impress, and inspire. Like McQueen's insect scene, without light and love, these antics offered empty emotional calories, yet they topped my menu—or, at least, the menu I allowed myself to see—and I consumed as much as I could, hoping they would fill me.

Both my boy Papillon and I learned that these things alone could not save us. I wish I could say I learned these lessons "soon enough." I wish I could. But it wasn't nearly soon enough. In fact, it was almost too *late*. The lessons themselves came soon enough; I just didn't *learn* from them, except maybe after the incident with Tarzan and the tow truck. And even then, I didn't fully grasp the lesson it taught; I just realized there was a lesson out there, somewhere, that I needed to learn.

Later in my life, a guy named David Neuman told me, "When the student is ready, the teacher will appear." David was a voice of reason during the stormy years that lay ahead, and I'll formally introduce you to him in a few pages. But, for now, I want to stick with what he said to me, and how, in hindsight, I can reframe my mistakes.

You know how we might tell our friends something, but they don't listen, then, years later, someone *else* tells them the same thing, and this time, they *do* listen. David's "When the student is ready, the teacher will appear" nails this phenomenon: We think we know it all, no matter what anyone tells us—the student isn't ready—but then, life points out a few cold, hard facts, and we take a few knocks, become open to change, and that's when that same advice becomes relevant; hence, when the student is ready, the teacher will appear. One domestic example might be: no matter how many times we are told as kids to wear sunscreen, no one wants to wear it until they've been burned a few times and realise, ah, yeah, that's a good call.

Over the following few pages, I'll share another lesson I needed to learn, but this student wasn't ready; not then, and not for nearly two more decades. Until then, I drank my dirty water with disproportionate and inappropriate zeal, while living a life that was deprived of light, and on half rations of love.

The lesson was that life in the fast lane can land you in the ditch. I wish it were a metaphor.

* * *

Real, lasting joy comes from within. The happiness I felt when I landed the Gyminny Kids gym was genuine, but after a few months, it became my day job. Liz was always the steady captain, and Rob was always the kind coach. I did well and gained their trust. I also gained confidence in partying on Friday nights and still being able to get my shit together for Saturday morning gym coaching sessions.

"Everyone works Saturdays," she'd said the day I met her. "It's the busiest day. If we let people choose, nobody would pick Saturday, so it's not optional." There was no ambiguity in her words. And for a while, there was no ambiguity in my understanding of them. But over time, I tested the limits. One such Friday night, around the end of November 2004, I challenged them to their breaking point, and, true to style, I did so in a cheap leopard-print loincloth.

It was Halloween night, and I was dressed as Tarzan. In my defense, it was a fancy-dress party, but I wasn't there for the costumes or the company; I was there to drink, heavily, and buy cocaine. That was the mission, and somewhere between 2 and 4 a.m., I handed someone the money and got what must have looked like cocaine. It checked most of the boxes—white powder, in a small, clear, tied-off baggie—but was, in fact, laundry detergent.

At the time, I'd drunk so much that I couldn't tell the difference. My nose was so burned out from my lifestyle that everything just felt numb anyway. I convinced myself that maybe there might still be a little real coke in the mix, so I snorted it all. I'd been drinking nonstop and now had an entire party's worth of Tide Pods in my bloodstream. My head felt like it was full of broken glass and bubbles, and I still thought I could drive.

Soon enough—yeah, unfortunately, it's more applicable here—I was on the I-56 in San Diego, doing 110, trying to get to my brother's. (I knew I was doing 110 because that's when the governor on my Explorer kicked in. That was the benchmark for danger: the moment the machine itself tried to tell me I was living too fast.) Anyway, soon enough, (again,) I reached my exit—a circular offramp—and took it doing twice what it was designed to handle.

I fishtailed hard, lost control, managed to slip through the only gap in the guardrail, and flipped over, and over, and over. The car rolled down the ravine, spinning through the ice plant, finally coming to rest on its passenger side, deep in a ditch, with me still somehow strapped in the driver's seat.

One thing addicts are experts at is justifying their habit, and I was no exception. I was drunk out of my mind, and limp and loose as the car did cartwheels, flopping back and forth like a rag doll in a washing machine, and for a while, I managed to convince myself that it was the booze that had saved me, as in, "Had I been sober and tensed up, I would have snapped."

Completely delusional.

Regardless, I was alive, in the car, stuck sideways in a ditch, but able to move. I crawled out of the passenger window, climbed on top of the wreckage, and leaped down onto the soft dirt. Apart from a few cuts and some friction burns from the seatbelt, I was fine. Still dressed as Tarzan, I took off into the night, running like a madman. I was barefoot, half-naked, bleeding, terrified, and rocking the leopard-print, with my heart still going 110.

I got to my brother's, woke him up, told him I'd flipped the car, then kept drinking through the night and into the next day. Maybe it was medicinal at that point. I'd taken a physical beating and should have taken an emotional one, too.

That came a few days later.

The police eventually found the car—totaled and abandoned—and somehow tracked down my parents, asking about the car and the driver and warning them that, although no body was found at the scene, the damage looked bad and blood was on the dash. That's when my dad called me.

Yeah, that was a rough conversation, and it wasn't the only one.

I also told Liz and Rob; I had to explain my absence on that Saturday. I explained that my clothes were scattered along the freeway and that I needed help retrieving them. At the time, I was homeless and living out of my car, so, in one night, I managed to total my home and scatter all my earthly belongings as well as dozens of Gyminny Kids t-shirts across a 200-yard stretch of the I-56. And after all that bullshit bravado, facing mortality, defying Death, and terrifying my parents, the thing that finally broke through my emotional Kevlar was Rob's offer to help me pick up my stuff.

He drove me back to the site a few days later, parked off the shoulder, and climbed down the ravine until we started seeing socks, underwear, and Gyminny Kids shirts scattered all over the ice plant. Rob didn't say much, but I could feel his disappointment. I deserved every ounce of it and then some. But regardless, he helped me gather the shredded dignity dotting the hillside, on which Gyminny Kids was printed.

Ironically, while I grew up resentful of not receiving love I felt I deserved, that day, in the ice plant down in the ravine, picking up dirty socks and Gyminny Kids t-shirts, the thing that broke through my emotional armor and finally touched my nerves was the compassion Rob showed me that I knew I did *not* deserve.

I cried hard.

The Explorer ended up in a tow yard. I still have a picture of it. The entire back of the car was crushed, and the roof was pancaked down to the bumper. The only part of the car that wasn't destroyed was the driver's seat.

I shouldn't have survived that crash. But somehow, I walked away with a few cuts, some glass in my skin, a belt burn, and another scar on my story. There's no logical way to explain it except by grace, luck, or maybe a stubborn guardian angel who wasn't ready to give up on me yet.

Down in that ravine, down in the depths of my humility, there was my lesson to learn, staring down at me from the gap in the guard rail. Through my tears, I saw Rob and Liz, along with some of the Gyminny kids I coached. I saw Steve Butcher, my parents, and my siblings. I saw Melanie, and I saw my own future kids, and a six-year-old girl in pink princess pajamas. They didn't speak; they didn't need to.

And next to me stood Death, inviting me into its clutch.

But I was a cocky bastard.

I acknowledged and defied it, challenged and dared it. Death and I were like two assholes in a bar, squaring off and saying, "You and me, outside. Let's settle this right now, one way or another. Let's go."

If I were going to kill myself with booze, drugs, and emotional sabotage—which I'd finally accepted was a scenario I'd bet money on—I was not going to do it in front of Liz, Rob, Melanie, and those gym kids; I was going to take it outside.

Three weeks later, I was gone, off to settle it outside, one way or another.

off axis

/ˈɒf ˈæksɪs / *adjective*

---

1 Rotating outside the line of control, risking instability, poor landings, and catastrophic failure. 2 A drift in mid-air, when motion continues, but the center and grounding are lost.

Chapter 6

lost in the rotation

/ˈlɒst ɪn ðə rəʊ ˈteɪʃən/ ***adj. phrase***

A disoriented state mid-spin where axis and ground are no longer distinguishable. Not a technical term—more a feeling shared by those who've gone off-axis. Recovery depends less on sight, more on instinct.

Part of me ran from San Diego out of shame. While I *could* keep doing this to *myself*, I could *not* keep doing it in front of the people who, for whatever reason, refused to stop loving me. How many times must a person apologize without changing their behavior before the words lose their meaning, and *trust* is irreparably damaged?

Part of me ran from San Diego to duke it out with my inner demons. The "You and me, outside, now" thing was subconscious, of course, mostly. It manifested as the party version of rolling up my sleeves and committing 100%. I've mentioned before about my two inner gorillas—the one who struggled to fit in and the one who struggled to be authentic. They had grown too big to coexist; I had to let them go at it, and like a good parent, I had to be fair and give them equal opportunity to express themselves.

And part of me left San Diego in search of adventure and opportunity. I felt I had outgrown my hometown and craved a bigger stage on which to perform. Because that was what I thought I was: a performer who thrived on attention.

And where could I—a young, photogenic (or so I was told) Southern Californian guy with abs, charm, endless energy for parties, and an insatiable need for attention—go to get my fix?

The answer lay 125 miles north, straight up the I-5.

* * *

Los Angeles—the *angels*—will make you feel like a god on Friday nights, but they will make no promises about how you'll feel come Sunday morning. That's not entirely true; they make plenty of promises, all of them exciting, and precious few of them genuine. If the angels tell you they'll meet you at the diner tomorrow morning, reserve a table for one.

Los Angeles was my kind of town, where promises made by night were promises broken by dawn. I've heard it said that you never get a second chance to make a first impression, and LA doubles down on this cliché. In Hollywood, you'd rarely get a second chance unless the first was especially impressive.

And that was my thing: I made a statement. For better or worse—or, in my case, for better *and* worse—I had a talent for showmanship, all for the price of a kidney and self-respect.

I kept my ID in my wallet, along with my memories and any sense of time. And I must have left my wallet on the bus or at the 24-hour Taco Bell because I cannot, for the life of me, piece this next chapter of my life together in any logical order. Perhaps I kept logic in that wallet as well. But just as Rob and I returned to the scene of my car wreck and found Gyminny Kids T-shirts scattered all over the ravine, I'll now go back to the scene of the train wreck of my life in LA and see if I can find my identity. All this happened between 2005 and 2010, between the ages of 20 and 25... I think.

Sorry for the mess. I promise I won't do it again.

* * *

There was this time, not long after I arrived in LA—fresh meat, naïve meat—when I started modeling. I paid a photographer to take some headshots and hired a stylist, along with a hair and makeup artist, to help me look the part. (I felt like a star just sitting in her makeup chair.) I got some decent headshots, which ended up landing me an agent. The agent then got me some runway work and modeling shoots, some of which were published in magazines, and that's when the train left the station... and immediately derailed.

The magazine photos led to invitations to VIP events and nightclubs with people whose names appeared everywhere in the city, from billboards to Billboard. I quickly gained access to dance floors, mansion parties, clubs, substances, and people. I partied hard, brushing shoulders with celebrities, climbing socially while simultaneously spiraling personally. I was on the fast track to impress, imbibe, and implode. I was broke, addicted, unstable, and unstoppable.

There was this time, at a mansion party, when a famous rapper poured champagne onto someone else's head like it was holy water. Another time, I was on a rooftop in Hollywood, watching two actors snort coke off a fruit platter while debating Nietzsche. One night, I ended up at a house in the hills where someone handed me a pill and said, "This one makes your trauma feel like a TED Talk." I took it, of course. I forgot the TED talk, but still carry the trauma.

While I owed back rent on a shitty Santa Monica Boulevard apartment, I lived deep inside the Hollywood nightlife, from dive bars to rooftop parties to sprawling mansion rages thrown by A-list directors. In LA, you can run into anyone on any given night: megastars, reality TV leftovers, faded names desperately clinging to relevance, and jackasses like me, doing backflips on the dance floor, trying to impress them all and losing my wallet countless times in the process.

Loosened up, hyped up, and regardless of what cocktail of substances I'd chased, I usually ended up wanting to dance. And more than that, I wanted to flip. Back tucks in the middle of nightclubs became my party trick. I was that guy.

I'd be drunk, sometimes barely able to walk straight, but I could still land a perfect standing backflip on a grimy bar floor. I was good. Years of gymnastics had hardwired that movement into me. I'd flip, the crowd would cheer, and just like that, free drinks would start showing up. I felt like gold in those moments—or a circus monkey—and traded tricks for validation and Jack Daniel's. It was perfect... almost.

Right before I did my thing, I'd hand my phone, keys, and wallet to some random person in the crowd, or toss them on a nearby chair or table. Then I'd do my party tricks. Then came the attention, the free drinks, and the invitations. Then there were the follow-up bar hops, maybe a Taco shop, and maybe even back to someone's apartment. By the time I thought to check my pockets and found them empty—sometimes hours later, sometimes days—the trail was cold.

Some nights I lost just my phone. Other nights, I lost my entire identity. And it wasn't like I had a backup plan. Half the time, my keys weren't even *to* anything. I might've been crashing on someone's couch that week or living out of my car, or sometimes just nowhere at all. I had a cheap scooter or motorcycle for a while, so losing my keys meant I'd be stranded, sick, and stuck somewhere I didn't belong.

The worst was when I'd finally crash from the weekend and realize I couldn't even get inside the place I was staying, with no phone to call anyone and no wallet to pay for any*thing*. All I had was my sick, broken body wandering the streets, trying to figure out where to sleep and where to throw up.

And then there was the Andy Dick incident.

peel off

/ˈpiːl ɒf/ **verb phrase**

To involuntarily lose grip mid-skill and fall away from the apparatus. Usually caused by miscalculation, fatigue, or loss of connection. Falling is part of learning. Regripping is part of survival.

I'd always thought Andy Dick was hilarious. For those who've not heard of him, he's an actor and comedian who's been in, like, *everything*. He's also been in-*to* everything. Don't worry (as if you *were* worrying); this is no potential slander case I'm setting myself up for. Pop over to his Wikipedia page and check out his legacy. There's nothing in this book that doesn't conform to the well-established, well-documented, and sometimes even well-*prosecuted* legacy of this LA sideshow. The guy worked hard to accumulate such a comprehensive and diverse resumé of chaos, and the following pages offer just a glimpse of life in the *Andy* lane, and on this occasion, where it intersected with life in the *Daniel* lane.

And I should add that, in this book, Andy represents many a mid-weeknight interaction. I tell this story not because it was unusual but because it wasn't. And not wanting to inundate you, I had to pick just one. Nor do I want to come across as name-dropping. The reality is that, back then, LA was where most film and TV was made. In San Francisco, there's Big Tech. In DC, there's government. And in LA, there's Film and TV. It's everywhere. Seeing someone you'd seen on TV or in movies was standard fare. Plus, once you've read the story, you'll see this had nothing to do with name-dropping.

And, to that end, I'm not even saying it *was* Andy Dick. It *looked* like him, and I *wanted* it to be him, and, with this being Hollywood, it *could well* have been him. But, then again, with this being Hollywood, it could well have been the guy who looked like Will Ferrell the previous week. You get my point. In my state, I have no way of knowing for sure. But, for the sake of keeping things simple, let's assume it was him.

Andy Dick played roles in some of my favorite movies—*Old School* being a standout one Melanie and I bonded over during our teenage years—so, being new in town, the first time I saw him at a dingy little bar near where I lived, that was cool.

Ok, now buckle up.

That "cool" quickly shifted to a kind of chaotic energy even *I* wasn't prepared for.

Andy was usually known for being, and often close to, blackout drunk; often seen staggering around, hanging off strangers—mostly men—and eventually being thrown out of wherever he'd wandered into. And this night was on track to be nothing special... for him.

But, being a fan of his, it was special for me, so I approached him with the wide-eyed enthusiasm of a young guy still impressed by Hollywood fame. We started talking and joking around with a loose group of others, and all seemed cool until Andy became aggressive. He was hitting on me hard, groping me, laughing, and getting a little too handsy. (Perhaps that's how he got his name.) Unsure if this was just some wild "bit" he was doing or if he was serious, I kept laughing and pushing him away. The boundaries were blurred. Everything with Andy felt like it could either be a joke or something darker *disguised* as one.

You know when someone makes a cutting remark and then dismisses it as "just a joke," or blames the recipient of the insult and suggests they need to "lighten up"? Andy's antics had that same ambiguity of intention. But eventually—and inevitably—Andy harassed one too many people, exceeded even the most charitable B-list tolerances, and he got kicked out of the bar along with me and some other random dude.

That's how the evening started. We levelled up.

From there, Andy flagged down a cab and insisted we go to the Roosevelt Hotel in Hollywood. I knew that place well; it was a celebrity hotspot. I'd filmed a "Pink" music video there and had been blacklisted from the place more than once for my own outrageous conduct. Of course, that didn't stop me from sneaking back in, usually to hang out at the pool. I didn't regard being blacklisted as a "ban," per se; more like a "conversation starter."

Anyway, in the cab, the Andy cabaret show kept going. He was sitting squished between me and that other random person, and without warning, he shat his pants.

I shit you not.

He squirmed in the seat, and the cab filled with a thick, nauseating odor of a middle-aged man's loose bowels. At first, I thought it was a joke—something over-the-top to get a reaction—but the smell. Oh my god, the smell. I was gagging.

When we pulled up at the Roosevelt, Andy, of course, didn't have any money to pay the driver. Neither did I, of course. I'd figured he was rich and famous enough that somehow it wouldn't matter, but no; he simply took off, running. And, of course, so did I. And, of course, so did the cab driver.

I ducked into a bathroom to hide—and to pee. (Just because my hero, idol, and on this occasion, my co-conspirator, dispensed with such a quaint formality of going to the bathroom to go to the bathroom didn't mean I could, too: I needed to pee and I needed to go to the bathroom to do that. It's just the way I was raised.) Andy followed me in and, for reasons known only to him, started laying into me, punching me hard and repeatedly, in the head and torso. And I returned the compliment. And that's when the cabbie found us. His challenge at this point was like some absurd arcade game: to grab our wallets while avoiding the flying limbs and not slipping on the stuff coming out of the bottom of Andy's pants.

We levelled up.

With the cabbie situation dealt with—neither of us had any money left—and the bathroom boxing match fading to an anticlimax—neither of us had any *energy* left—Andy's son turned up out of nowhere and drove us to a rundown house not far from Hollywood. It was a crash pad; nothing but some mattresses thrown down on the floor. That's where Andy was living at the time.

Exhausted, creeped out, sad, bruised, and yep, without my wallet, phone, keys, or ID, I asked his son for a ride home, and thankfully, he agreed.

Just another Tuesday night.

That was just one of several run-ins I had with Andy during my years in LA. He was insanely smart, outrageously funny, and completely out of control—a living example of how easy it is to get swept up into the madness when you're young, drunk, and desperate for excitement in a city that feeds on bad decisions.

* * *

There's one more LA incident I want to share—for now—that I believe marked a turning point for me; not for what happened while I was out, but for what occurred after I got home.

I was living just off of Santa Monica Boulevard in Hollywood in a crappy apartment, and I was broke. I was always broke, always two or three months behind on rent, hanging on by less than a thread—I couldn't even afford the *thread*. The only reason I wasn't out on the street was that the building manager had a soft spot for me. She was a sweet lady and would actually lend me money to help me catch up on rent so I wouldn't get evicted. Who does that? I'd pay her one month when I owed three, promise to catch up the next week, and the cycle would continue. That's how I lived for a while, floating between lies and desperation, charity and calamity.

One night, after a particularly exhausting, coke-fueled bender—during which I lost my phone, keys, and wallet—I made it back to my apartment, crawled through the kitchen window, and lay on the cold kitchen floor. I was sick—so sick—not "hangover" sick or "vomit" sick; I was, like, deathly sick: the kind of dehydrated, poisoned, hollow feeling that makes your soul want to quit.

I hadn't eaten anything in nearly a week; not a bite, not a thing. I tried to sip water from the tap, but I couldn't even hold *that* down. I was throwing up bile, shaking, and barely able to move.

After a few days of crawling between the kitchen and the bathroom, I finally gathered enough strength to get off the tile floor in search of something to eat. There was nothing in the apartment—no money, no cards, no food, no phone—just a few crusty condiments in the fridge door: nothing but a black, rotten banana on the counter.

This was my *Papillon* low.

The thing looked like death—as, I am sure, I did—but it was the only option.

Desperation is a strange thing. That banana, I swear to God, was the best thing I've ever eaten. It tasted like hope, and for a moment, I forgot how sick I was. I just sat there on the tile floor, chewing and remembering what it felt like to eat.

My body wasn't ready, and the first bite came right back up. So I slowed down; paced myself. I nibbled that rotten banana for six hours—six hours—just trying to keep it down, little bite by little. And eventually, I did. It stayed. It was the first thing I'd eaten in days.

That rotten banana, as banal as it sounds, became a symbol for me: On the one hand, it was a symbol of degradation. I realized I'd been living like an animal—a degenerate—with no food, no hygiene, no direction; only rot, lies, and wasted life. Yet, on the other hand, I was grateful for it; it gave me something to hold onto, something to slowly digest, something to think about, something to keep me going just a little longer—long enough to repeat the cycle a week or two later, perhaps, but also long enough for me to finally crawl to my first AA meeting.

pommel horse

/ˈpɒməl hɔːs/ *noun*

*A padded, handle-topped training apparatus used for
continuous circular motion. Mastery comes from repetition,
rhythm, and navigating imbalance. Falling off is common.*

Much like the first time I drank a beer, back when I was 12,
my first visit to an AA meeting wasn't a big deal for me. No
applause, no fanfare, no pat on the back, but also, no filters,
and no bullshit—just a folding chair, burnt coffee, and a few
people trying to stay alive, trying to stay sober, trying to stay
human.

There was one guy there who looked like he hadn't slept
in a year, who said the most honest sentence I'd ever heard: "I
didn't think I was worth saving." I wrote that one down.
Another woman, dressed in bright colors, said, "Don't leave
before the miracle happens." I wrote *that* one down, too.

I didn't think I was worth saving, and I needed a miracle:
self-worth and miracles—where do you find those things?

These people seemed to believe it was a multi-step process—twelve, to be exact—but being the go-getter I was, I wanted it to happen faster than that.

I didn't get sober the first time I tried, or the second, or even the seventh. I sincerely quit drinking hundreds of times, usually around 7 am, after waking up and screaming into the toilet bowl, only to be drunk again by noon *that same day*.

See, addiction has never felt like a choice to me. It might have looked like one to others, and I understand why they'd see it that way. No one forced me to drink; I went to the bar, I bought booze or drugs, I drank or snorted them, and I justified my actions. But, for me, it never felt like a *choice* I was making.

For me, it felt like gravity, a force of nature. For me, pain resided not in the consequences of my drinking but in the effort it took to resist. Like a rock climber hanging by his bleeding fingertips on the slimmest ledge, the pain of not drinking—the effort of holding onto that tiny ledge of self-worth—became so overwhelming that it consumed all my thoughts. And when I couldn't hold on anymore, I'd let go, and afterward, I'd free-fall, and gravity would do the rest. That's how it felt for me.

There have been many times in life when I've asked, "Why me?" Why can others drink without this tractor beam locking onto them? I could have reframed that. I could have asked myself, "Why *not* me?" or "Why aren't I dead already?" But then I'd have to ask why I wasn't born with some motor neuron disorder, or as a refugee in some war-torn country, or murdered and left in a ditch when I was a kid. None of this is in our control. And if I asked these questions, I'd have to start being grateful.

Why me?

Why *not* me?

Everyone has their own burdens. If I had taken a moment to consider all the terrible things that *could* have happened to me but *didn't*, I might have seen things differently. I might have realized that, to some people in the world, being a young, good-looking (or so I was told) gym coach living in LA, with friends and family in San Diego—with or without a drinking problem—might represent every hope, prayer, and dream they've ever had. I might have realized that perhaps one billion people in the world could only wonder what my kind of privilege must be like as they struggle for survival under circumstances that are completely out of their control. But I didn't take a moment to consider such things. I focused, instead, on what I *believed* others had that I thought I deserved and was unjustly denied.

Whether or not this delusion—this mental illness I had—counts as "no fault of my own" is moot. What's not up for debate is that it was—and remains—my burden to carry, my responsibility to manage, and my fault if, for whatever reason, it hurt others.

Of course, it's easy to say these things in hindsight, and it's always helpful to remind oneself of gratitude and personal responsibility, but back in LA, I wasn't there yet. I was deep in self-absorption, and as hard as I tried in AA, it seemed there were a few lessons I still needed to learn and fully own before I could get a foothold.

And as I've said before, when the student is ready, the teacher will appear. By this point, I was ready.

* * *

I was living in some run-down place in Hollywood on the corner of Crack and Whore. For those who haven't been, Hollywood, as a *brand,* is glitzy, but as a *neighborhood,* it's quite different. Some of its streets are more "cracky," and some are more "whorey." You get the picture. So, I was living there, or couch surfing there—I'm not sure. Neither am I sure what would have been worse: having nowhere to go and having to ask to sleep on the couches of those who chose this place to live, or making the commitment to put down my roots here myself.

But none of that matters much in this story, beyond a little context.

Anyway:

I got on an LA Metro bus—maybe headed to a meeting I wasn't planning to stay for or a job I was about to lose—and found a seat toward the back. I hunched into my hoodie, popped my headphones in, and slunk down, doing my best impression of someone who didn't exist.

A woman sat down right next to me—mid-40s maybe, or mid-60s, it was hard to tell—and on this crowded bus, we were touching shoulders. She had a hollow look, her skin like paper, her eyes sunken and vacant. In the bag on her lap was a bottle, barely hidden in a crumpled paper bag. I didn't want to look at it. I didn't want to look at *her*. In truth, I didn't want to see *myself* in her. I couldn't *not* see myself in her, so I looked down at the floor.

Without warning, she suddenly lurched forward and began vomiting.

Sidebar:

* * *

I want to take a moment to let you know that this part of my story, along with many of the previous ones, may be gross to you. I want to assure you that this is not the point. It is not my aim to simply offer a gratuitous stream of squirm- or gag-inducing content that may or may not entertain or repulse you. I have better things to do than that, or to do *without a higher purpose*. My goal is to sit beside anyone who has also sat in this seat on the bus, is currently sitting in it, or thinks they are heading there.

In many ways, I look back on this bus ride as a metaphor for life. I felt helpless, gross, and out of control, out of touch with my direction, on a route others were also navigating. While I did find a certain sense of community—whether with the AA community, the bar scene, or the drug scene—we were all on the same bus, headed for the same terminal. None of us was in control; all of us felt helpless. At the speed we were going, few of us realized that getting off was even an option.

Okay, end of the sidebar and back to the story:

* * *

This woman started vomiting, and not delicately or with any sense of self-awareness or communal consideration; she was beyond that. On this crowded city bus, she was very much alone in her suffering, isolated in her ability to connect to anything beyond her body's physical rejection of the lies she'd been consuming for who knows how long. The rancid contents of her stomach hit the floor with a thick, wet slap like pancake batter—yellowish, runny, chunky. And the smell was unreal; sour and stomach-turning. At that point, three things hit me:

The first and least offensive thing to hit me was the puke itself. It splattered all over my shoes, soaked into the cuffs of my jeans, and crawled up my shins like hot shame, as if I'd pissed myself in public. But, whatever.

The second thing that struck me was my annoyance at what I thought, at the time, was an unnecessarily over-dramatic response by other passengers. But, then again, drama *was* what LA was known for. I watched, almost pathologically detached, as people around us jumped up, gagging and cursing. One guy yelled, "Jesus, this is why I fucking hate public transportation," while everyone else moved away from us as if we were lepers. Had they never seen puke before? But again, whatever.

The third thing that struck me was my proximity to her, not in a *physical* sense, but more critically, in terms of my *narrative*. And following that thought, I was struck by my lack of motivation to distance myself from her *physical* proximity. It was as if I were in this mess too. I was.

I sat there, next to her, frozen in place and drenched in her bile, not out of shock or kindness—fuck, no, I didn't try to help her; fuck that. No. I sat there because I knew, deep down, that I wasn't far from where she was in her storyline. I *was* her, just a few pages behind. Maybe even just a few lines behind. I had been that sick. While it wasn't *me* who puked on *this* occasion, it *could* have been me, and it might *still* be—I couldn't rule that out—and if that *did* happen, I would have had a similar lack of self-awareness and consideration for others.

I sat there because part of me believed I deserved her as my fellow traveler and had earned her as my guide. We were, in many ways, passengers on the same bus in life. If I wasn't yet in her seat, I soon would be. It doesn't take a medical degree to see how unhealthy we were.

And as these three things hit me, they also, in their own way, began to soak in and permeate my senses: the contents of her stomach began to soak into my clothes; the judgment of, and rejection by, a repulsed society began to soak into my ego; and the message that the moment was trying to teach me began to soak in to my awareness: we were both headed for oblivion... unless I got off the bus.

When I woke up at the City of Angels Medical Center, less than a week later, after saying "just one more," and was told my heart had stopped the night before—meaning I'd been clinically dead—I knew it was time to get off the bus.

The paperwork I received sounded like a dark joke. The doctor's advice was to "Discontinue the use of cocaine," which I found both blindingly obvious and tone-deaf, and I laughed when I read it. But then again, it was given by someone who was thriving to someone who'd been clinically dead, so who was I laughing at?

Is there a level lower than clinical death? Not that anyone has returned from.

Yep, if I wanted to get off death's bus ride before it reached the terminal, now would be the time. I knew this would likely be the last stop; my last chance, and no one else's choice but mine to do so.

coach's hand

/ˈ kəʊʧɪz hænd/ *noun*

An unseen or lightly guiding presence during risk. Rarely forceful, but always intentional, and it is often all it takes to prevent a fall.

The point in my story where I went to the ER, stopped breathing, and was pronounced clinically dead for a minute seems like a good time to give everyone else a breather, too. It's been bleak. I want to point out that I might have been unfair, so I will take a moment to clarify that life wasn't all bad.

While the previous chapters might have appeared to have left no room for daily life, there was, in fact, a daily life. I *did* manage to make it to the supermarket *occasionally*. I *did* manage to find places to live, *occasionally*. And I did make contacts.

David Neuman was one such contact.

And I did seek work, and occasionally, I brought in money that allowed me to pay rent, renew phone contracts, replace lost phones, buy clothes, shave, do my laundry, and so on. I wasn't *"homeless"* homeless, but I did couch surf. I wasn't jobless; I bounced from job to job, securing some for longer than others. And while some work was barely more gym-related than what I might have found if I'd waited outside Home Depot, some Gym owners offered me coaching gigs. These jobs went well until I let them down one too many times, and then we'd all move on.

Anne Josephson was one such owner.

* * *

David Neuman is the *"When the student is ready, the teacher will appear"* guy *I* mentioned earlier in the book. He was a network television executive and someone I now consider a mentor. He didn't try to fix me; he just stayed close. While most of my friends wanted to party, David wanted to chat.

We'd hike Runyon Canyon three to five times a week when I wasn't too hungover to make it, and when we weren't walking, we were eating dinner and talking philosophy. He'd gently—but clearly—push me toward the version of myself I hadn't yet learned to believe in: someone meant to work with kids, to lead with integrity, to live clean. I didn't always take his advice—*"When the student is ready, the teacher will appear"*—but I heard it, and I will never forget it. He even confronted my party crew once, telling them point-blank: "If you keep partying with Daniel, he will die—and it will be on your hands." Some of them pulled away after that. David never pulled away.

David cared enough to have the difficult conversations. He believed there was something divine at work in this journey—that I was meant for better things. He once told me that my energy had a way of attracting good things—even when I was too lost to see it—and that, with the right focus, that same energy could save me.

He was right.

The truth is, I probably wouldn't have made it through LA without him.

Anne's importance in this story is equally critical but arguably more tangible.

I was deep into my addiction, but despite having that hollow-black-eyed, jittery look, my body was still capable of some gymnastics, and Anne took a chance on me; she gave me the benefit of whatever doubt there might have been in her mind. Whether her misgivings were centered around her trust in me personally, or stemmed from weighing her hiring options in general, she took a chance on me, and it paid off— until it didn't. My soul was completely off balance, and sure enough, I began showing up late, then missing shifts, then disappearing without explanation, until eventually, I left her with no choice but to do what any business owner would do—or had already done: she let me go.

At the time, I blamed such fallout on others—anything but myself. That was my pattern: create chaos, disappear, and shift blame. In most cases—nearly all my interactions, in fact—when others saw me as unreliable and inconsistent, they reasonably concluded I was a bad employee and decided to cut their losses. But Anne was different. She knew something even *I* didn't fully understand; I wasn't a "bad employee," I was an *addict*.

This is a critical distinction.

I have a friend who was recently diagnosed as an adult with ADHD and dyslexia. He'd struggled with self-worth his entire life. He couldn't understand why he felt he had so much to give, yet couldn't make anything land. People told him to work harder, focus on one thing at a time, make lists or spreadsheets, and offered every other technique to fix what was not even the problem: barking up the wrong treatment. But even just learning that it was ADHD made everything click. No wonder he'd started project after project, business after business, relationship after relationship, only to lose interest. His whole life, he'd been trying to treat the symptoms—or worse, the *assumed causes* of those symptoms. But when he learned the cause was ADHD, it all made sense.

He wasn't a failure; he had ADHD. In his own words:

"It was like, in a world of cats, all I wanted to do was chase squirrels and chew on bones. Throughout my school and adult life, I was met by cats who would judge me as a bad cat, a *failed* cat, and chronic judgment wreaks havoc on self-esteem. But when, out of the blue, someone says, 'No, man, you're a *dog*. What you do; that's what *dogs* do,' that changes everything. What's even more interesting is that I saw that the coping mechanisms I'd developed in trying to be a masked dog conforming to cat rules weren't all negative. Plenty *were*, but some were really positive. I was creative, funny, and energized. I wasn't a bad cat; I was a brilliant dog. If I could shake the low self-esteem, I'd be okay."

Yes, my friend was poor at organization, and yes, he was brilliantly creative. Once he understood why, he started outsourcing the organization and focusing on his creative work, as well as being open about who he was; he began to thrive.

And that's what Anne did for me. Instead of dismissing me as a bad employee—lazy, or an asshole, or unskilled, or disrespectful—she saw me as someone with a serious drinking problem. That distinction was a game-changer. Anne was the first person who convinced me to call myself an addict and seek help for my addiction.

When the student is ready, the teacher will appear. That's when it clicked.

* * *

I don't remember what happened the night or days before my death—yes, I just wrote that—but I do remember laughing at the "discontinue use of cocaine" summary provided by the doctor. And I recall Anne reaching out to me a few days later, after she heard, and saying the same thing, just with different words. She didn't have to reach out; she had every reason not to. Yet she told me quite directly, without judgment, and with compassion.

"Daniel, you are an addict. Your addiction will kill you. You could be, and still can be, a great coach—a coach who could change thousands of kids' lives—but only if you overcome your addiction to the substances that are destroying your body."

Then she offered to pay for outpatient treatment—not because she owed me anything or because I'd earned it, but because she saw a flicker of something worth saving.

That kind of grace cracked me open. It didn't fix me—not immediately, and not directly—but it planted a seed suggesting that while I might have appeared to be "the problem," the cause was not *me*, per se, but *inside* me like some kind of psychological tapeworm consuming my self-worth and stimulating my need for, well, stimulants. This is not meant to be a denial of responsibility—it was, and still *is*, my duty to fix—but the nuance stopped me from blaming my soul for the fault within the system that is my psychological makeup.

I sometimes go out to buy clothes. I might find a shirt I like, try it on, look in the mirror, and think, "It's not me." I sometimes shave, then look at whiskers in the razor and wonder if those whiskers are still me, or if they *ever were*. I look at my hands, read about amputees, and wonder if our limbs are really us. Can I lose or swap a limb and still be myself? My limbs aren't me. What about our hearts? Are our hearts really where our identity resides? Not according to heart transplant recipients. What about our minds? Don't we have free will? I'm not even sure our thoughts are ours. We've all been influenced (or under the influence), and we dream, or have irrational fears. Are these ours to own? I'm not convinced. Hear me out:

You might be reading this right now, hanging in there, wondering where I'm headed with it, and suddenly, a thought might cross your mind. You might think, "Did I pay the electricity bill this month?" or some other seemingly random thought. Was that idea really yours? Who, or what, authored that particular thought? Where did that pop-up idea pop up from? Because not one second before, you were right there with me. Was it *your will* to have that thought pop up in your mind while you were reading? Because if it *were* your will, that would have required you to have known what you wanted to think *before* the thought occurred to you to think it. It's a contradiction. More likely, the thought was generated somewhere upstream from your "will."

The point is, I believe we have much less control over our thoughts than we'd like to believe. More personally, I had always thought "I" was the problem. But after Anne labeled the "problem" as "addiction" and believed in "me" as a "coach," her grace opened me up and created a divide between these two gorillas (remember them?) duking it out inside me. One—the good one, the "me" one—had talent, potential, and self-worth, while the other—the asshole one—was wounded, a parasite, a psychological tapeworm, a disease inside me, a mirage. The revelation was, *they were not me.*

I was ready, and the teacher appeared. The lesson was that I was an alcoholic, and alcoholism is a *disease I had*, not an *identity I was.* Yes, it was my responsibility to get well, and the actions—and damage caused by them—were mine to control and repair, but much like my ADHD friend, just the diagnosis, just the word, switched something in me—away from blame and toward the potential for forgiveness, redemption, and rebuilding.

I accepted Anne's offer. I completed the outpatient program. I stayed sober for a while.

But addiction is patient and cunning. I relapsed again. I got a DUI. I disappeared again. Yet still—still—that moment with Anne stuck with me. I couldn't shake it. That's the thing with good, reasonable ideas; it's impossible to stop believing them. It was one of the first times in my adult life that someone truly invested in me without expecting anything in return. She saw "me" through the smoke and did not confuse the person with the disease. As a result, I started to do the same.

Looking back, I can say with certainty that David and Anne were the first crucial glimpses of light on my road to recovery. Their kindness didn't heal me, but it softened me, opening me up to the idea that I was not the disease; I was its *host*. It made it harder to hate myself completely. It made it harder to believe I was unworthy of help or that I was beyond hope.

Without obligation or ulterior motive, they reached back and extended their hand to someone they saw drowning. Maybe they were paying it forward; our reasons are personal. Years later, when I've had the chance to give someone else a second shot, to reach back instead of moving on, I think of them both. I think about how someone with enough courage and compassion to look beyond the theatre of daily interactions and see the person in front of them as separate from their behaviors can change the course of a life.

Los Angeles—ironically, *"The City of Angels"*—had been hell for me. Many thrive in LA, and many suffer elsewhere. It just so happens that my story is set in California, so, for me, LA had been a city of personal fires and internal riots. But after much torment with my demons, I had met my angels. If the "discontinue-cocaine" doctor had pointed out that Death was in the hospital waiting room, sipping coffee from a vending machine, and looking for cheap wins during the ER late shift, David and Anne were the angels who opened the curtains. They let in the light, separated "me" from my disease, offered a helping hand, and gave me hope.

And if there's one thing Death despises, it's hope.

I had run away to LA to wrestle my demons out of view of the people I loved.

It was now time to head back to San Diego, to face my demons, precisely *because* of the people I loved.

roundoff

/ˈraʊndˌɒf/ **noun**

A redirection skill that sets up something bigger. Begins like a cartwheel but ends facing forward. Used when backward motion is needed to build forward power.

After five years snorting LA and throwing it up, trying to get my asshole demons to work it out between them, Anne's act of grace—or charity, or faith, or even foolishness, depending on how you feel about me right now—gave me the tools I needed to develop a clear spiritual mission and plan for San Diego. But as difficult as it was to start this next yellow brick road, it was still only the beginning. I knew I still had all my work ahead of me.

I was broke, broken, and out of options, and everyone knew it. I'd burned bridges, flaked out, relapsed, and vanished. I wasn't someone most people would hire, or live with, let alone trust around children, not given my history with addiction.

It had been years since I'd left her, since I just walked out on her. I had disappointed her in so many ways. Our stories went back so far, and I believed deep down that we had a future together. I was sure she'd found someone else since we'd "lost touch," and I prepared myself for her rejection and the ire of her partner. But despite all this, I felt compelled to try reaching out. It may sound rude and even reckless, but I believed we could become a family; grow a new family, start fresh—and I was driven to try.

She had every reason to say no, and sure enough, when I knocked on her door out of the blue and asked her to give me another chance, her partner lost his mind. They had a full-blown screaming match, with voices raised and things thrown. He was furious. He was livid. But she stood her ground, as she always did, and told him this was her decision.

She said yes.

Liz said yes.

I'd gone back to Gyminny Kids, knocked on Liz's door, and asked if I could work there again, and Liz said yes.

It's more complicated than that, of course. Rob hadn't seen me since the two of us hiked down to the ditch below the off-ramp of the I-56 (where Tarzan had totaled the Explorer) to help me pick up dozens of Gyminny T-shirts that had been scattered like Catherine wheel sparks from my car. And while Liz initially said yes, she was actually calling my bluff, and as usual, she was right. I backed down, realizing I wasn't ready. Nonetheless, that "yes" planted a seed in me—proof of concept, if you like those kinds of marketing expressions—that redemption was possible.

As long as I did the hard work of getting sober.

* * *

After five years snorting LA....

I'd burned bridges and vanished....

It had been years since I'd walked out on her....

But despite all this, I felt compelled to try to reach out to her....

I believed in my heart that we had a future together....

I believed we could become a family....

But she said yes.

Melanie said yes.

Yes: *Melanie!*

Barefoot-on-the-trampoline Melanie.

The *"that-kind-of-girl"* Melanie, who was one of a kind.

The Melanie who got me when no one else did.

The girl who wore the t-shirt that read, *"I'm your future—brace for impact."*

Yeah, *that* Melanie.

She said yes.

We'd known each other since childhood, when we were little kids tumbling together at the YMCA in San Diego, long before life got complicated. We lost touch during my lost weekend in La La Land and reconnected when I returned to San Diego. She had two beautiful kids from a relationship that didn't quite work out, and, well, some flames never die; some relationships seem to float above the mundane. She was steady, kind, and utterly uninterested in the chaos I was used to bringing into people's lives, and equally uninterested in tolerating that kind of behavior in her own. I loved her, and she had a very pragmatic, "I love you, too—go clean up your shit" perspective. And she still wore that T-shirt. Somehow, we fell in love, and somehow, she said yes... with caveats.

As long as I did the hard work of getting sober.

* * *

Two strong women, two beautiful kids, one new job, one motherfucker of an addiction that turned into a no-holds-barred, bare-knuckle—and white-knuckle—mud fight, and one last chance.

San Diego is a border town. If you keep going, you cross the border. It's also a beach town. If you don't stop, you're in deep water. But if you do stop, put down roots, work hard, and love with an open heart, I'm not sure what's more golden about the place: the sun, the sand, or opportunities in life.

But, again, it's on the border. All it takes is one wrong turn.

The symbolism could not be more apt.

I had one more chance.

As long as I did the hard work of getting sober.

* * *

Liz had seen something that day when I knocked. Maybe she just saw the kid I used to be—the one who loved gymnastics, made the kids laugh, and had potential buried under layers of pain. Despite Rob's understandable apprehension, Liz was stubborn in the best way.

"I know he'll pass on it," she justified to Rob, reassuring him that I wouldn't take the job. "But he seems different this time."

She was right; I did pass, and I was different—not fixed, but fixable. I reached out again after a few mostly successful and always painful slogs through AA, and at that point, they could see I was sweating it out.

You see this kind of thing when coaching kids in the gym. After you've coached for a while, you realize that there's no clear link between the talent a kid demonstrates when they start and how they end up. As a coach, and essentially a kind of talent scout, we look for the kids who sweat it out; we look for the kids who, regardless of their ability on day one, get back up after every fall, no matter how bruised they are. We look for the ones who brush it off and step back onto the mat. I was always that gymnast. And I was always that coach. Maybe Liz saw that in me now, in life. I kept getting back up. Maybe Melanie saw that in me, too. Because, after two decades of training hard, coaching hard, and drinking hard, I always got back up.

Rob came around slowly at first. He was cautious, and I don't blame him for being that way. I'd be the same. He watched me work, saw me show up early, stay late, and hustle with a smile, doing whatever it took to get the job done. And, over time, I earned his trust, not through words but through consistency.

And Melanie did the same.

We'd always had an incredible understanding of each other, and as we reconnected as adults, we had more to say. We were more able to strike a deal.

When I saw her, I felt I'd returned home. She was my other half. And the two kids she had now elevated the stakes. She was now a mother, and this resonated profoundly with what I wanted in life: to be a father. I'm *really* good with kids, and she knew that, could see that I would be great with them, and *for* them. And I loved them instantly.

Not only did I see Melanie as my other half—my soul mate, for want of a less trite expression—but I also saw the bigger opportunity of being a dad. She knew this, and, well, wasn't opposed to the idea of having me—or more accurately, the *best parts* of me—in her life, again. Plus, being in her early twenties and a single mother of two wasn't optimal. Her options were to work and not be a parent, or to be a parent and not have a dime. And Melanie was born to nurture.

Then there was me: a ravenous, if misaligned, energy monster with no clue how to manage a home life, but with the skills and passion for coaching kids, and a desire and compulsion to work and be part of a family.

We both saw that, in addition to our natural "soul-mate" connection, there was something bigger here. We were like two jigsaw pieces that, with a few tweaks, could be a perfect fit.

As long as I did the hard work of getting sober.

So, Melanie and I had some tricky, adult conversations about what would need to happen for this to work, and we struck a deal:

Melanie would parent, and I would provide.

If that meant coaching 50+ hours a week at Gyminny, plus private lessons, flipping items at garage sales, driving Uber in the early mornings, and starting a leotard brand from our kitchen table, so be it.

Another rule was: no drinking in the house. She was, and is, a practical person. She knew I had a problem. She didn't say no *drinking*; she said no *drinking in the house*. While that differentiation might sound like a pedantic, childish manipulation of meaning on my part, it wasn't. Melanie knew who she was dealing with, wanted the benefits of our potential relationship, *didn't* want the drawbacks, understood which parameters were within her control and which weren't, and was clear about her boundaries. This wording of hers was a form of tacit permission for me to scratch the itch she knew tormented me, and a clear boundary for me not to cross when scratching it. I understood the rules. She understood the rules. And we both understood the line in the sand and the consequences if that line was crossed.

And she said yes.

And I said yes.

And we got married in 2011 and had three more beautiful kids between 2012 and 2016. Five incredible gifts. Let me tell you about them:

Audio, as it happens, is passionate about music, power, and impact. He's taken gymnastics and life head-on with courage and fire. Watching him grow into a man has been one of the greatest privileges of my life.

Axel is my warrior. He taught me that fatherhood isn't about biology; it's about consistency. He trusted me to guide him since we met, when he was two years old. I've never taken that responsibility for granted. His resilience and spirit inspire me every day.

Finley, you've already met; she's my baby gorilla. She's fierce, funny, radiant, and wise beyond her years. She's seen me at my worst and still loved me without conditions. That kind of love changes people. It changed me.

Remi's quiet strength and deep sensitivity remind me that the most intelligent people in the room are often the ones who speak the least and listen the most. His heart is pure gold. He protects his siblings and observes the world with thoughtfulness. He taught me how to listen.

Rocket's physical gifts are just the beginning. What makes him so special is his joy for life, his humor. He makes every room brighter. Rocket is the bright dressing on our mixed salad family.

You might be thinking, "Dude, you just arrived back in San Diego and now you're married and father to five kids. Did I, like, miss a season?"

No, you didn't miss a season. However, I feel that now is the time to restate that, having always wanted a family, Melanie and her first two children inspired in me the tangible realization that she was moving forward with her future, and I had been invited to join her, as a family man, albeit with some conditions. There was an opportunity for me to be a family man. I want you to be aware of how fundamentally important family has always been to me, and I can think of no more open and honest way to do that than to introduce my kids to you.

So, no, you didn't miss a season.

There was never really a doubt that Melanie and I were meant for each other, or that I loved kids and wanted a family, or that I wanted to build a business and provide for them. Never a doubt. The doubt was whether or not I could get my shit together. And once we reconnected, discussed ways to make these two jigsaw lives fit and work, and established boundaries, we went for it.

Being with Melanie came with conditions—family—and in this moment of saying yes to each other, I was saying yes to the two already kicking up dust in the yard, and three more who were soon to join the party.

On a superficial level, this book is about the recovery, redemption, and transformation of one guy. On a deeper level, it's about the universal takeaways discovered along the way. But above all—most important of all—this book is about kids: how vulnerable we can be as kids when we don't know who we are, how powerful we can be as kids when we speak the truth, the joy of parenting and coaching, and witnessing—and *experiencing*—growth, energy, laughter, and transformation.

In many ways, at this moment in my life, when saying yes to Melanie, I, too, was still a kid. But not quite in such a cute way. There's a concept that's discussed in some of my addiction meetings that claims that we stop maturing when we start drinking; that addicts use to duck the mirror and avoid the challenges that make adults adults. And I started drinking at the age of 12. If this theory is correct—and I have no reason to believe otherwise—I was still immature. Some of that immaturity came out in positive ways—I was a great coach, I got kids, I was creative, I was fun—and, of course, some of it came out in horrible ways.

Let's get back to the story:

After Melanie and I got married, I worked 80 to 100 hours a week for seven straight years, without taking a day off. All the while, we stuck to our understanding: Melanie held down the home front, and I did whatever it took to provide. I missed birthdays, milestones, middle-of-the-night feedings, first words, and quiet moments on the couch because I was either out working or out using.

Yep, recovery isn't a straight road, at least it wasn't for me.

Sometimes, I told myself I was sacrificing for the family, while other times, I knew I was just running from guilt. There were moments when I'd promised Melanie I'd come home and then didn't, and times when I lied straight to her face and then disappeared for days.

My psyche was like the Wild West during the gold rush; I saw opportunities that needed diligence to nurture and safeguard—the family—and I wrestled with rogue elements—

my demons—taking them outside for duels, often returning injured but determined to keep going. Melanie's genius was that she neither pitied nor pandered to my drama. We had simple rules and boundaries, and as long as they were honored, it was up to me to do my job, dust myself off, and get back to work.

There's gold in them hills, and to get it, we need tools and the desire. Without those, forget it. But even with them, that's just the beginning. Next, we have to climb the hill, then dig and dig and dig. And then—just maybe—if we're lucky, and patient, we'll strike gold.

That was the plan, at least, *as long as I did the hard work of getting sober.*

tucked position

/ˈtʌkt pə ˈzɪʃən/ *noun*

A compact body shape with knees to chest and arms wrapped inward. Reduces risk, shortens rotation time, protects the core. Often, the instinctive shape when preparing for impact.

There's no off switch with the slugfest that is addiction and recovery, only steps in the right direction; tools, routines, connection, honesty, and surrender—things I once believed were signs of weakness.

In retrospect, I see that recovery, at least emotionally, shares similarities with gymnastics, resistance training, and even life itself if we want to succeed. We work until we fail, then we work again, which feels awful, and we fail again until, eventually, we quit and let gravity reclaim us.

However, if we keep on getting up, going back, and doing the work, progress is made. It might not seem like progress—struggle, failure, struggle, failure—that's a tough slog with no obvious room for joy—but if we tracked some elusive metric of recovery, it might resemble a wild, unpredictable, and jagged zigzag line trending upwards.

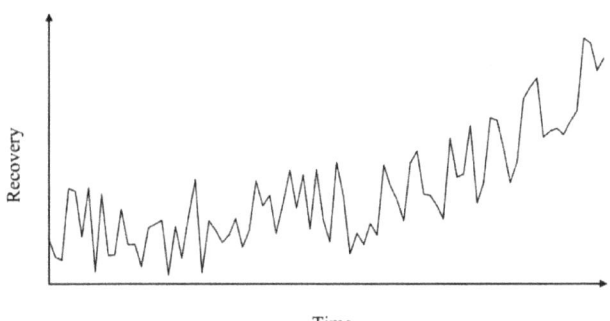

In these cycles of work and failure, I found that, ultimately, joy would be perpetually elusive if regarded as permitted only beyond some arbitrary finish line. Because there *was* no finish line, there *is* no finish line, and there *never would* be. In life, love, business, recovery, or even training for an event *with* a finish line, there is no finish line, because, if there were and we crossed it, *then* what?

Indulge me for a second:

I've sometimes imagined life as a sequence of moments, like squares on an endless Chutes and Ladders board. To find joy, maybe we need to surrender to the game. Of course, we hope for the ladders—wins in sports, or business, or love, or recovery, or life—and we try to avoid the chutes—losses in those same things. But shit happens, and sometimes it happens on the roll of the dice. Whatever our position in life at any given moment, there's no square on this endless Chutes and Ladders board—no moment in the game—that doesn't have a square behind it in which things could be worse, and does not have a square in front of it where things can be better.

It's anyone's game. It's everyone's challenge. Where we start is arbitrary, and what happened last year—or last week, or yesterday, or a moment ago—doesn't matter. What's important in this and any other moment is accepting that things *could* be worse, things *can* be better, and that it's always our intention to move in the right direction when we take our next step. If we can find peace with that, and even joy in the absurdity of it all—because what other choice do we have— that can't be taken away from us.

I can't say I was able to find joy in my relapses. On the contrary, they were filled with shame. However, I kept playing the game. I kept getting up and going back to the mat. I kept doing the work, and progress was made.

* * *

Melanie and I had reconnected slowly and carefully. I was still struggling with addiction, trying to rebuild a life from the ruins. She wasn't naive—she saw the mess for what it was and understood that progress would be uneven. But she also knew that as long as I followed the rules and kept my side of the bargain, there would be an upward trajectory. As I battled the ups and downs, she saw the bigger picture.

Melanie's boundaries were clear—no drinking around the kids. So when I relapsed, I disappeared. Not because I didn't love them, but because I was ashamed. I didn't want them to see me like that. That was the bottom line, the golden rule.

Don't let the kids see you like that.

We had children together before I was fully sober. I wasn't clean—but I was trying. And she knew the difference between trying and pretending. We didn't just fall into a relationship. We built it—through counseling sessions, late-night arguments, long periods of silence, and even longer spans of grace.

And for the record, the bumps in the road, the relapses—the chutes—were not pretty.

And there were two distinct chutes that stood out as waterslides from and to hell. These two moments were similar in that they were lapses, yet they were different incidents, and they impacted me in very different ways.

* * *

The first happened around 2017.

I'd left on a Friday and didn't come home until the following Tuesday morning. That bender nearly killed me. When I finally walked through the door, I felt spiritually bankrupt and physically wrecked, sick beyond words. We lived in a three-story condo at the time, and reaching the third floor felt like climbing Everest. Every step was a fight. When I finally got to our bedroom, I collapsed into bed and started spiraling through withdrawal—heart palpitations, shallow breaths, cold sweats, and confusion. I could barely stand. I crawled to the bathroom just to sip water from the sink and then lay on the floor, too weak to get back to bed.

At one point, I stood up too quickly and threw up into the bathroom sink. (I didn't have the strength to make it to the toilet.) It wasn't just liquid; it was thick, chunky bile from days of drinking with no food, just stomach acid and whatever was left inside me, which wasn't much. I tried to run water to rinse it down, but it clogged the drain. I couldn't fix it, so I lay back down on the floor in my underwear, dizzy, shaking, clinging to life and hoping I wouldn't die right there.

When Melanie came home later that day, the sink was still full. She looked at me, didn't flinch, didn't scream, didn't cry. She just restated our agreement.

"I'm not cleaning this up. You need to clean it up before the kids see it."

Border town.

She didn't say it with malice or as a threat; she said it with stoic pragmatism.

But I couldn't clean it up. I was too weak. So it stayed in the sink for another day and a half while I lay there, trying to breathe, trying not to vomit again. And the whole time, Melanie just went on with her day—getting the kids to school, running the business, folding laundry, making dinner, stepping over me.

Stepping over me. That was the worst part; she *stepped over* me. If you ever want to feel small, put yourself in a position where people can step over you.

* * *

The second chute—the second incident of a lapse that stood out to me—was profound in a very different way. I already told you about this, earlier in the book, but I'll tell you again, because, this time, I wasn't stepped over; I was laid down next to, and looked at in the eye, by Finley, my then six-year-old daughter, (this was July 2020) and asked straight up, with the innocence of an angel, why I hadn't taken care of my responsibilities.

"Why didn't my baby gorilla put me to bed last night, like you promised?"

This wasn't another adult with an agenda, or an opinion, or the ability to step over me; this was a little girl, with no agenda, no opinion, no clue, no understanding of why her father was letting her down.

I'd left my clothes at the front door after a three-day bender. The mix of alcohol, cigarettes, sweat, and shame had soaked so deep into their fabric that it made me nauseous. I peeled them off and stumbled through the house as the sun was coming up in nothing but my underwear, and collapsed on the living room floor, face down on the carpet. I couldn't make it to the bedroom. I didn't have anything left. My body was done. My soul was sick. My underwear was wet.

And then I heard her voice.

"Why didn't my Baby Gorilla put me to bed like you promised?"

I hadn't heard her walk in. Finley was standing over me, freshly awake as the sun peeked through the living room sliding glass door, and the dust particles danced in the sunlight. I didn't look up. I couldn't.

I didn't say a word. I *wanted* to, but I had no words left. I was all out of excuses. After 23 years, I'd run dry.

Finley didn't step over me; she lay down *next* to me, looked her dad in the eyes, and asked why, and then waited for my answer as our tears soaked the carpet together.

I recalled my life at her age, feeling the shame of failing my parents' definition of success. It stung. I recalled the slow dimming of the light and hope in their eyes, and how empty that left me. And so, I avoided them.

And I recalled, as I grew, this self-loathing poisoning my self-image. Despite a tenacious work ethic, "charm," and talent as a gym coach, I recalled the shame of failing my own definition of success and saw the slow dimming of the light and hope in *my own* eyes. And so I avoided them, too, through work.

Yet, worst of all, on this day, I watched the same fading of hope in my own child's eyes. And as Finley looked at me that morning, asking why her baby gorilla hadn't tucked her in like he'd promised, I saw that same hope fading from *her* eyes.

I tried to avoid them. I tried to close my eyes. But I couldn't. They were my baby girl's eyes. My baby gorilla's eyes. I tried so hard to force my eyelids shut so I could slink back into the dark and dodge the spectacle of shame and humiliation. But I couldn't.

My addiction had so far failed to kill me, and I had failed to kick it. As yet, my rock bottom had not been defined. So, ever in search of the depth of my soul, my addiction forced me, via some Clockwork Orange-esque ambush of the ego, to look into my daughter's eyes, in a moment of profound humiliation, and answer for myself.

Twenty-three years before, I'd started drinking to avoid my demons.

Then I'd run away to LA to let those demons duke it out.

Then I'd returned to San Diego to face them, hoping to sweat them out.

But never did I know why I had such demons.

But as Finley looked into my eyes and asked, "Why?" this was the exact moment I finally asked myself that same thing:

"Why?"

There are moments in life, on the endless Chutes and Ladders board, that contain chutes that send you plummeting, and there are others that contain ladders that allow you to climb. And they each have squares behind them in which things could be worse, and in front of them, where things could be better. But in this moment, for me, this square felt like a universe all on its own. There was no past or future; things could not possibly be worse, and recovering from this was beyond my imagination. There were no chutes and ladders in this moment. This square was like a portal into I don't know what. But as I stared into her eyes—unable to turn away, unable to answer her simple question, and unable to answer mine—I felt my soul burn under the scrutiny of the moment. And I felt the noise of life fade away, and the complexity of the world fall into focus.

Because, after 23 years of questioning my value, my worth, and my purpose, in this vignette of abject humiliation, the answer to all my questions was staring me in the face, and all she was asking for was for me to tuck her in.

It was that simple.

the dismount

/stɪk ðə ˈlændɪŋ/ **verb phrase**

The final move in a set routine where the subject releases from the apparatus and returns to the ground—ideally with precision, control, and grace. A moment of truth: where form meets finish, and preparation is tested by impact. Where we decide whether the pain meant something, and what kind of ground we want to land on.

kip up

/ ' kɪp ʌp/ **verb phrase**

*A skill that transitions from hang to support using minimal
momentum and maximum timing.*
*Not about strength alone—about knowing when to push. A rise
that doesn't look like effort but demands much work.*

Finley wasn't the only baby gorilla in my life. Gyminny Kids
needed tucking in, feeding, and nurturing, too. I wanted it to
grow, and with Liz and Rob kind of "parenting" this one, I
could focus on what I do best: coaching. And every kid at the
gym was a baby gorilla too—swinging and jumping, and
screaming with joy and sometimes crying with frustration.
But in this jungle, I was able to get all the endorphins I needed
and actually serve the community.

I have tried on numerous occasions throughout this book
to effectively express the unusually high level of innate energy
with which I have been both blessed and cursed. And it's that
duality I want to explore for a moment.

No blessing is entirely good, and no curse is altogether bad; traits are neutral and can work both for and against us. Sometimes, I think that our mission in life is not so much about discovering our strengths and weaknesses, but about acknowledging our most potent driving force. Because even the biggest wrecking balls, when swung in the right direction, can achieve incredible things. Every sword is double-edged, and one man's terrorist is another man's freedom fighter. You get the point.

If, and when, we discover our most powerful driving force, even during times of self-destruction, we should acknowledge its strength. My wrecking ball, my double-edged sword, my "most potent driving force" was my energy. For others, it might be people-pleasing, or intellect, or dedication to their art. More than just my energy, I had the ability to push my body to its limits, over and over and over again. And beyond that, I could inspire others to join the Daniel party.

In its darkest form—the form in which I had no direction or purpose—this double-edged sword, the terrorist within me, gave me the energy to stay awake for four days straight, while drinking myself to death: surviving for years on zero calories as I couchsurfed from failure to failure, shame to shame, broken promise to broken promise.

Yet, in its brightest form—the form in which I found direction and purpose—this double-edged sword, this freedom fighter within, gave me the energy to stay awake for days without stopping, while working my ass off at Gyminny Kids, coaching them to reach their full potential; 100 hours a week, for seven years. It gave me the energy to not just survive but thrive on zero alcohol while watching our family flourish and witnessing Gyminny Kids grow from strength to strength; seeing all my baby gorillas grow stronger and stronger.

It was the same sword, but its purpose changed depending on who wielded it.

The Finley moment was when I began my real recovery. I checked into rehab, got sober, and remained sober. If I think of the Chutes and Ladders analogy, it's as if I decided to remove all the chutes and ladders from my life. I stopped chasing big wins and risking big losses. To make real progress in my journey—something I wanted—my chance-based approach had to end. No more chutes and ladders—just a clean board, focusing on one little step at a time, one manageable day at a time.

Life, love, recovery, rebuilding trust, building a family, or developing a business are all proverbial journeys of a thousand miles. Well, they are not even that; they are journeys with no finish line. They are works in progress, works *of* progress, and process, and of looking forward, no matter the setbacks, no matter what happened yesterday or a minute ago. They start with a step and continue, step after step.

There is a saying that goes something like: The best time to plant a tree was twenty years ago. The second-best time to plant it is now. And the one thing I learned in math that I found interesting was what's called proof by iteration. The idea is that, to prove an endless challenge can be overcome—and for this analogy, let's call it an infinitely tall ladder that must be scaled—we only need to prove two things: first, that no matter the rung we're on, we can always step to the next rung, and second, that we can reach the first rung.

It begins with a step and continues, one step at a time. No one can expect more than that. No one can do more than that. And no one needs to do more than that; just ask Neil Armstrong. Metaphorically, his actions represented a giant leap for humanity, but to him, personally, in that moment, it was just one more small step.

In life, love, business, and recovery, we should never underestimate the power of the first step in the right direction. And while the best time to have taken that step might have been 20 years ago, the second-best time is now.

* * *

I must have been doing 100 plus when I spun off the I-56 exit ramp. The car must have spun through LA for about five years, and even back in San Diego, it still spun. The noise, the effort, the mental violence visited upon not just my life but also on the lives of everyone I loved left a trail of destruction and landed me face down in a carpet-lined ditch, in wet underwear.

Finlay lay down next to me and looked into my eyes.

"What are you going to do?" she asked.

I sat up and looked around me—at the guard rail and the exit ramp, to Melanie, Liz, and Rob, who sat silently, watching. They didn't say anything. Finley had asked the only important question. I looked at the car; it was a wreck. I have no idea how I survived, no idea. I looked up at the I-56—dark, noisy, and cold. I looked at the exit ramp, then back at Finley. Finally, I looked at myself and then back at Finley.

"What do you want me to do?" I asked.

"I want you to come back," she said.

Then I looked up and saw Melanie, Liz, and Rob. They didn't say anything; Finley had already said what they wanted to say.

And so, I looked back at Finley again.

"Let's go home and get cleaned up," I replied.

"How?" she asked. "The car is a wreck."

"We don't need the car, baby gorilla," I assured her. "We can walk."

"How far is it?" she asked.

"I don't know, baby girl," I answered.

"How long will it take?" she asked.

"I don't know that, either," I said, "but here's what I *do* know: if we start walking right now and keep taking one step at a time, in the right direction, the sun will rise, and together we'll make progress. Is that okay with my baby gorilla?"

Finley nodded, stood up, and walked back to her bedroom.

I slowly got up and shuffled over to the front door, picked up my clothes, and put everything in the washing machine. Then I shuffled into the shower. Then I shuffled to the kitchen and made breakfast for Melanie and the kids. Then I shuffled to work. After work, I shuffled to AA and then rehab.

I shuffled for days.

I shuffled for weeks.

I shuffled for years, until it didn't feel like shuffling anymore.

And sure enough, the sun began to rise.

* * *

At first, I was just coaching recreational classes—sweeping the floors, spotting cartwheels, folding mats. But I kept showing up. Every day. On time. Sober. Grateful. And gradually, they entrusted me with more responsibility.

And as they slowed down, I stepped up, initially as a coach, then as head coach, and finally as the gym manager. Then, one day, Liz pulled me aside and said something so bittersweet, I can still taste it.

"Rob and I have started thinking about retirement," she said, "Y'know, cashing in; selling the business to someone who can take it to the next level. And we thought of you."

"Liz," I replied, looking at her like she was crazier than I was, "I don't think I'm the right person, plus, I have a family of seven to feed. I'm not in a position to buy or run a business."

"I know," she smiled, "and I assumed you'd pass on it. Okay, no problem, I just thought I'd ask."

But somehow, I knew she wasn't acting like this was the end of the conversation.

"When?" I asked. "When were you thinking of...?"

"Oh, not anytime soon," she smiled again. "A few years, maybe. Certainly not before we find someone who has the heart, the work ethic, and the vision to take Gyminny Kids to the next level; not before we can teach them the business; someone who loves gyms, and kids, and coaching."

"But I already have all that," I protested before realizing I was being set up. "I see what you're doing, Liz, but I wouldn't even know where to start."

"How about we start small," she suggested. "You're already our head coach and pretty much manage the place. How about you start making all the executive decisions? Just for a day. Let's call the position, oh, I don't know, 'chief executive officer' or something silly like that?"

"You want me to be CEO?" I was confused.

"You look confused, Daniel," she said. "What part of this do you find confusing?"

"Liz," I protested, "I'm a recovering addict with no money and no college degree."

"I know," Liz nodded. "Okay, if Rob and I got struck by lightning right now, who do you think would be the best person to run Gyminny Kids starting tomorrow until the perfect CEO is found?"

"Me, I guess," I replied.

"I agree," she nodded. "There is no one who comes close. You have the heart, the work ethic, and the vision to take Gyminny Kids to the next level; you know the business; you love gyms, kids, and coaching. The rest, you can learn. I believe you are the ideal candidate for the job, and it appears that we share similar instincts when it comes to selecting CEOs. That's a huge executive decision, and you handled it perfectly calmly. You might even be cut out for this. I'm going to act on your advice. You're hired. Thank you, and I'll see you tomorrow."

I was sitting at the kitchen table, as pale as a ghost, when Melanie and the kids got home that evening. She'd seen that kind of fear in my eyes before, but never had it been accompanied by such a smile.

"What happened?" she asked.

She'd asked that question of me many times before, but never had it been accompanied by such a smile. And she looked as warm and golden and lovely as the San Diego sunrise.

I'd made her smile.

iron cross

/ˈaɪən krɒs/ **noun**

A rings hold requiring immense shoulder and core strength. Arms extended, body suspended—a test of stillness through tension. Rare, punishing, and reminiscent of spiritual transformation.

By now, you've probably realized that I was never meant for academic or corporate success; I was a damaged gym rat, rushing around in search of meaning. That said, one of my favorite stories is a modern parable adapted by the corporate world, called *Who Moved My Cheese* (by Spencer Johnson). It isn't an obscure book; it was on the NYC bestseller list for almost five years. No secrets here, or if there are, they aren't my ideas. They are inspirational, in my view, and help to tell my story.

In essence, *Who Moved My Cheese?* is about a few mice living in a lab maze who get used to where they usually find their cheese (i.e., sustenance, meaning, purpose, clients, joy, etc.—insert one's own desired "cheese" for relevance). One day, their cheese is gone—it's just not there—and the way the individual mice react to this news is the main point of the book; some get mad, and some get busy.

When our expectations are not met, some of us get mad; we walk in circles, cursing and yelling our objections along the lines of, *"What the fuck! It should be here. It's always here. Why is it not here? Who moved my Cheese?"* I'm sure we all know those people. And then there are those who take a more practical approach, along the lines of, *"Well, this drive-through is closed, so we should keep looking."* Because it doesn't matter *who moved our cheese*; what matters is *where we can find more.*

I think for the first part of my life, until the age of 12, I built up in me an unreasonable sense of entitlement. I was the first kind of mouse; I got mad. Worse, I was *Oppenheimer-Mouse*, secretly developing resentment—secret even to *me*—about what my purpose was and where I could find validation, until that resentment reached a critical mass. It should have been at home, or school, or whatever. The truth was, I couldn't find it, couldn't *express* that I couldn't find it, couldn't shake the need for it, and resented that hollowness that grew within.

And then, between the ages of 12 and 35, from opening that first can of Bud Light to being unable to explain myself to Finley, I was the other kind of mouse—the get-busy kind. In my case, *Oppenheimer-Mouse* might be a fitting name for *this* guy, too; exploding out onto the world with reckless force in the hope of ending my suffering, without nearly enough thought put into the fallout I'd cause and the people and bridges I'd burn.

And then there is my post-Finley-carpet moment, post-CEO-offer life, filled with purpose and direction. Yet this author still knows he is still Oppenheimer-Mouse and always will be, fully aware of the dangers of suppressing or misdirecting my energy. Indeed, a percentage of the motivation pie chart (or cheese wheel) for writing this book is dedicated to reminding myself of this fact.

Energy is neither created nor destroyed; it just changes form, and what form it takes is, to a large degree, something we can control.

MY MOTIVATIONS

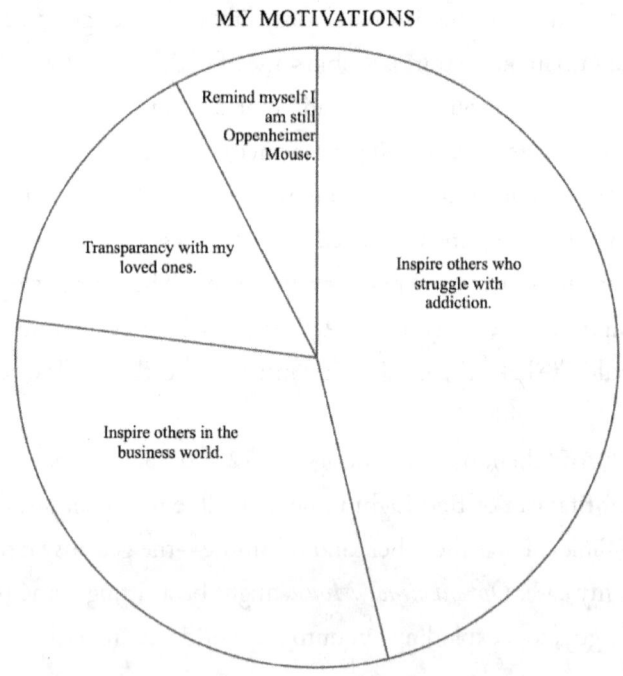

I often think back to the first time I met Steve Butcher and felt a sense of what I could become: a father, a coach, and an entrepreneur. Despite the chaos in my late teens, in LA, and even when I returned to San Diego, I struggled with my demons in pursuit of these goals. Now, some decades later, I've begun to see that vision of myself coming together.

Family and fatherhood, it seemed, were simple equations; if I gave love and care, I'd receive joy from seeing our family thrive. Coaching was no more complex: when I provided technical guidance and support, I took pleasure in watching the kids succeed in the gym. I also soon realized that entrepreneurialism—and, with that term, I include my then-new CEO responsibilities, because at the top of even the biggest corporation is an entrepreneur—was something I could grasp easily and make my own.

That's the thing about becoming comfortable in our own skin; we make it our own.

I'd always been *fake*-confident. The guy doing back flips on the dance floor was fake-confident. But after discovering an innate comfort in the gym and putting in quite possibly 100,000 hours of coaching, the business of gyms, kids, and inspiring them to be their best was something I understood down to my core. And after getting sober, with Liz as my guide, things really took off. Year after year, we went from strength to strength.

You know, when you learn to ride a bike, there's that moment when your parent or whoever's teaching you holds the saddle while you wobble all over the place, trying not to fall. That was Liz with me. But then there's that moment when things start to feel steady, and you begin thinking, "I'm getting the hang of this." That's when you dare to tell the person keeping you upright to let go, because you want to see if you can ride on your own.

"Let go," I yelled in excitement as I felt Gyminny Kids wobble less and less.

But Liz didn't hear me. When I looked back to see why, I saw her way down the road.

"I let go a while back," she assured me. "You've been running this place longer than you realize."

And that's the first time I realized that someone had pushed that pin back into the grenade.

Buying Gyminny Kids wasn't easy; it took a while. I didn't have a trust fund or investors. I built it step by step: one paycheck at a time, one lesson at a time, one bruised shin at a time, one step forward on the endless Chutes and Ladders board at a time.

We threw Liz and Rob a great retirement party at the gym. That day was also my first as the outright owner of the place. It was 2021. I was 36. The gym had taught me a few simple lessons in life, the most basic being: if you fall, get back up. In gym culture, there's usually someone there to reach out a hand and help you up. The other lesson I learned from the gym culture I grew up in was that if you saw someone else fall and you were the one standing, then you should be the one to reach out your hand. This egalitarian culture was ingrained in me as a coach, and part of my transition to becoming a CEO and business owner was to embody that same spirit as a leader.

* * *

Eli DM'd me on Instagram. He sent me a message from a sober living facility during COVID. He said he'd seen a Gyminny Kids ad and asked if we were hiring. He mentioned he loved working with kids and just wanted a chance to be useful.

I almost didn't open it. Like many messages, it got buried. But something prompted me to go back and read it, and his story hit me in the most personal way:

Eli had been homeless, living on the streets. He had relapsed countless times, lost everything, and developed a severe eye infection that went untreated until it left him permanently blind in one eye. He told me people mocked him during his lowest moments. Even other addicts laughed at him for talking about recovery, but he kept trying, kept praying, kept getting up, and kept following that crazy zig-zag line of recovery, always facing forward.

And that's how he ended up reaching out to me, by facing forward and taking a step.

I brought him in not because he had the perfect résumé—he didn't—but because I knew him; I was him. He was me. I knew what it meant to be seen despite our mistakes. And I understood how powerful it could be when someone said, "Yes. I will give you a chance."

Eli wasn't the first questionable person to reach out to me. When I lived on the corner of Crack and Whore, people would try to sell you anything or claim it was cocaine when it was washing detergent. I wasn't naive. And some of the sharks I've met in business are just as wily. The only difference between them is the products they are hawking. Cocaine or foam mats, insurance or accounting systems—these things don't sell themselves, and I've become a pretty good judge of character.

Eli started small in the maintenance department. Then he was promoted to coach recreation classes as he learned the ropes and took the feedback we gave him seriously. The kids loved him right away. He was so fun.

"How many 'i's in Eli?" he'd yell at the start of every class, with a smile on his face.

"*One!*" the kids would yell back, immediately realizing this guy owned it.

"You got *that* right," he'd yell back. "You guys are *good*. Now, how many 'i's in *win*?"

"*One!*" the kids would yell back, with mounting excitement.

"You got *that* right, *too*," he'd yell back. "You want to win with Coach Eli?"

"*Yeah!!!*"

At this point, even the new kids loved him, and the energy was about to burst.

"All those in favor, say Aye."

"*Aye!*" They'd scream with excitement now boiling over, ready for the signal.

"Alright, one lap warm-up. *Go!*"

And they were off.

Parents began requesting him, and our other coaches respected him. He's become one of the most beloved teachers in our program. Three years after he first reached out, he's now making an impact on over 100 kids each week.

Eli came to me a while back to be the one to give him his two-year AA chip. For those who don't know, it's an AA thing, and for the most part, I've kept the internal workings of AA out of this book. AA is meant to be anonymous, after all, and even if it weren't, the work done in the program isn't that interesting to those on the outside. Indeed, the work involved is irrelevant to us if it doesn't ultimately change how we do as recovering addicts as we interact with the real world.

That said, there are some beautiful and important milestones—note, I didn't say finish lines, I said *milestones*—that are recognized in the program, and oftentimes, those who reach these milestones ask key partners to join in the recognition, which temporarily relaxes the code of anonymity. Regardless, I asked for his permission to tell his story.

So, Eli asked me to give him his two-year AA chip. Naturally, I said yes, and with tears in my eyes and pride in my heart, I handed him the two-year token at one of his meetings—a token I had earned not too long ago.

"Because of you," he said.

I handed it right back, and I knew I was starting to sound like Liz when I said it, but I said it anyway.

"No, brother. Because of *you*: *You* walked in. *You* stayed. *You* showed up. *You* had the guts and the grit to stick with it. And how many 'I's in grit?

He laughed.

"I'd best keep hold of my one good one, then," he smiled.

"Don't worry," I reassured him, "If that one pops out and rolls off, we'll find some other word. How about courage?"

"I like that," he nodded, "It's got 'age' in it. What about 'guts'?"

"There's a 'U' in guts," I laughed. "We're covered."

"That's a win," he nodded. "It takes guts."

"You got that right," I mused, "You got that right."

* * *

Eli taught me an important lesson in life. On this endless Chutes and Ladders board upon which we live, there are always squares in front of us and behind us. The key I've learned is not to keep score or compare positions. We are never so low that we are beneath being offered a hand that reaches back, and we shouldn't be shy about accepting help from those who can lift us up. Likewise, we are not above being the one who turns and reaches back.

If it weren't for Melanie's, Liz's, or most poignantly, Finley's courage to ask tough questions, I probably wouldn't have taken over Gymimmy Kids. If that hadn't happened, some other owner likely wouldn't have hired Eli. As a result, there wouldn't be 100 kids a week out of their minds with exuberance as they warm up, running around the gym, knowing that the prize for first place is to be first to hang out with Eli again.

I learned that, no matter how small the moment or who extends their hand, every gesture that says "I believe in you, take my hand" contributes to an immense and complex human effort to lift us all up, help us progress, and find joy along the way.

Chapter 14

stick the landing

/stɪk ðə ˈlændɪŋ/ **verb phrase**

To finish with precision, presence, and control after a difficult routine. A moment of grounded stillness that says, I made it. Not about perfection, but about holding your ground—even if you wobbled on the way down. The art of ending strong, owning your story, and standing tall in the aftermath.

The title of this chapter is cute, but in some ways, it conflicts with my belief that there are no dismounts, no endings, or finish lines in life. But this is a story about transformation—a single chapter in the book of life.

We can all break our own lives down into stories. Whether it's a gym routine, or a day at work, a vacation, or raising kids until they leave home, we each live in countless simultaneous stories—long and short, grand and subtle—that are each destined to contain their own beginning, middle, and end, and that, combined, make up the complexity of the moment.

Many of these stories have already been finished. They can sit on a shelf, in a photo album, or live in memories, manifest as anger, or resurface in therapy sessions. Many others have yet to begin, and we can dream, wish, or work toward these goals. But the most interesting ones are those that have started but are not yet complete, and it is on the pages of these incomplete stories that life is ours to write. Because the truth is that we are not just the protagonists in these stories—passengers on their narrative arcs—we are the authors of our own futures.

What's done is done. What's yet to be done is yet to be determined. The only moment that matters to the author is what to say next. There is no word in any story that wasn't, once, the very next one to be decided, and at any given moment, that next word is ours to choose.

On the endless Chutes and Ladders board, it doesn't matter what happened last year, or last week, or yesterday, or a moment ago; what matters is that behind us is a square where things might have been worse, and ahead of us is a square where things can be better. There is no home and dry; only "What now?"

And that response is ours to author.

In the past, Finley asked me, as did Melanie: "*What now?*" *Do I want to be a husband and father, or not?*

Andy asked me, kind of, along with a thousand other LA encounters: *What now? Do I want to risk my life in the pursuit of a mirage?*

My addiction asked me on countless occasions, and still does: *What now? Am I okay feeling depressed or frustrated, or angry, or lonely, or should I take its medicine?*

Anne asked me: *What now? Do I want to die?*

Liz asked me: *What now? Do I want to challenge myself and grow the business?*

And I've asked them all, too.

"Are you going to love me?"

"Are you going to hate me?"

"Are you going to forgive me?"

"Can you ever trust me again?"

But in reality, for me, these were simply reflections of the questions I asked myself during all the moments in between, in the negative space between interactions and distractions; the most primal being *"What now?"*

"What now?" might actually be a better chapter title; it makes no judgment of the past. It stoically assesses the *now* and implies the question, "What's next?" as in, "Okay, and now what?"

After the incidents with Finley and Liz, "What now?" stopped being just a question I avoided and became one I asked myself multiple times a day. It served as a way to reset and remind myself that I was on a Chutes and Ladders board, and it was my turn. It became a form of mindfulness, helping me stay aware that I was the one making decisions in every moment. I'd tried avoiding that responsibility, and saying it nearly killed me is an understatement. It *did* kill me, for a minute or two, until people with training and the presence of mind to see my clinically dead body and ask themselves, "What now?" used high voltages and chest compressions to move us all into the next square on the board.

And as I started living this new way, asking "what now?" my path changed from avoidance to mindful decision-making.

Transformation is not an inspirational moment; it's a conscious process.

We do not "turn a corner," we navigate change.

Each day, I make a conscious decision not to drink.

Every day, without fail, I made that conscious decision.

Even *this morning*—yes, today, July 20th, 2025, the day I am writing the first pass of this chapter—as I collected my five-year-sober token, I felt proud of the work I've done, but I understand that one poor choice—or the absence of a good one—made tomorrow morning, this evening, or even in the next minute could undo everything. I remind myself that this token reflects the past, not the future, and has no say in the next decision I make. There's no room for complacency; I have to shape my future myself, one conscious decision at a time. If I value what I've built, I should consider my *'what-nows'* carefully.

Each day, I make a conscious decision to cherish my family. Every day, *without fail*, I make that decision. I found that gratitude and faith work well for me. For others, it may be different. To stay present and mindful with my family, I make conscious decisions daily.

In coaching, I've always been attentive and fully present. Coaching has always been my talent. I've been honest about my weaknesses, but for that to be a genuine assessment, I should also acknowledge my strengths. I've always been good at it, energized by it, and found joy in the moment while doing it. Any coach spotting a trampoline session who finds their mind drifting elsewhere should stop and go to that place elsewhere. As a coach, I was always in the zone, and as a head coach and CEO, if I ever saw one of my coaches spaced out, not paying attention, or complacent—their mind elsewhere—conversations were had.

And as a CEO, every day at work, I carefully considered each what-now with the same seriousness and sobriety with which I can only assume those ER medics had as they handled their responsibilities during the day that death temporarily claimed me.

And it took years. I didn't have a trust fund or investors to help me buy Gyminny Kids. Not at first. But each day, I asked myself, *"What now?"* and made conscious decisions in the right direction. I rebuilt my self-esteem, one meeting at a time, one "what now" at a time, one paycheck at a time. Indeed, a couple of years ago, I was able to purchase the gym from Liz and Rob, give them the retirement they deserved, assume sole ownership, and continue their legacy.

Ownership.

My Motivation

Taking ownership is perhaps even more fundamental than asking "what now?" Maybe that motivation pie chart might look more like this...

Because taking ownership of a business is one thing, but taking ownership of mistakes is another.

* * *

There were years when my marriage was more about survival than romance. Melanie and I had an unspoken, then a spoken, agreement: she would raise the kids, and I would work like (good) Oppenheimer-Mouse to provide for them. It wasn't balanced for either of us, but it was all in service of the future we wanted. I was obsessed with creating stability, financial security, and a future. She held down the fort with five kids and has been there for them 24/7, 365 days a year.

None of this is possible without Melanie. She's the anchor—the one who kept believing when I didn't, the one who saw past the addict, the workaholic, the fear, and the flaws. She raised our kids while I built the company, and she patiently helped nurture the version of me who is present, sober, accountable, and loving.

Today, we talk daily about our goals, family, and what matters most. We walk together. We laugh. By the time this book is published, our five kids will either be teenagers or very close to it. That's a full-time job—five full-time jobs—but there's an ease between us now, a joy, because we built it with our own hands.

I'll never be able to repay Melanie for the second, or third, or fiftieth chances she gave me. But I try every day, starting with a *"what now?"* in the morning and ending with a *"thank you"* in the evening.

* * *

I've been transparent about my lows. I'd like to be no *less* transparent about the wins I've experienced. That was the deal I made with you at the start of this journey: honesty on all fronts. And that includes the salacious *and* the rebound.

In fact, this was the whole point of writing this book: not to beat myself up—I'm done with that—or hope to earn royalties from book sales—I'm doing okay financially—but to share my experience that, no matter how low we feel, our story is not over, and we are its author. There's hope. There's always hope.

As I stand on my current square on this endless game of Chutes and Ladders, I see my chaotic past: a demoralized kid unable to find a clear way to direct his energy, a reckless son, a thoughtless employee, and a talented coach struggling with a drinking problem. I see my mom's hijacked Maxima and my crumpled Explorer. I see Andy Dick, rotten bananas, and bus rides to the ER. I see Death's face and Anne's grace, bathroom tiles and carpets, and I see golden smiles. I see a hand reaching out to help me up, and I see myself through the eyes of a child.

And in this moment, I see an incredible wife and five amazing kids. And I hold a token commemorating five years of sobriety.

Close to my heart, I've seen success in business; Gyminny Kids has expanded to four locations, employing over 100 staff members. It is now a two-time *Inc. 5000* honoree and an eight-figure business. This success has enabled me to be more philanthropic in the community, founding the Coaches Cup and raising over $150,000 for nonprofits like St. Jude's, Make-A-Wish, and Rady Children's Hospital, as well as donating half of my real estate commissions to child-focused charities. I've generated significant social influence and impact, including a six-figure monetized YouTube subscriber base.

Closer to my heart, I enjoy live public speaking events where I discuss topics such as health and well-being, business, gymnastics, and addiction and recovery.

And closest to my heart, Melanie and I have been married for over 13 years, raising five kids who are not only thriving but also high-level athletes: Rocket is now competing as an elite/Olympic hopeful, and our two oldest boys are competing at level 10 with college aspirations.

I stand here as a person transformed.

Transformed by faith from hopeless to limitless.

Transformed by hard work from self-loathing to self-made.

Transformed by a higher calling from user to provider.

Transformed by the love of a woman, a child, a mentor, and an employer, to become the husband, father, mentee, and business owner I'd dreamed of even before my first Coors Lite.

And in the squares in front of me? Well, I've learned not to look too far into the future. The most important step in life, for me, remains the very next one I plan to take, so I keep my ambitions modest.

So, what now?

Tomorrow, I plan to show up.

Tomorrow, I plan to do the right thing.

Tomorrow, I will walk into gyms with my name on the deed, speak at leadership events, sit across from lawyers, accountants, and my advisory board, and own my decisions, even as the memories of sleeping on vinyl couches while hugging my backpack, terrified someone would steal my stuff, still permeate my consciousness.

Tomorrow, I will check my defenses to ensure I don't allow the mirage of addiction to corrupt my vision, and I'll do this not by gazing at the horizon but, rather, focusing on the solid ground right in front of me.

However, even before that, I have work to do this evening, so if you don't mind, I'll sign off for now. I'm off to say goodnight to my kids. It's been a while since even my younger ones wanted to be tucked in; they are a bit too old for that now, but they're not too old to be reminded how much their dad loves them. And then I'm going to sit with Melanie and tell her how much I love her. She's not too old to hear that either. She's had a long day, and I want to make sure that if she needs anything, I'm there for her.

the beam

/ðə biːm/ **noun**

A narrow apparatus demanding balance, composure, and complete presence. Success depends not on perfection, but on recovery after the wobble. A shaft of light that cuts through dusk—revealing dust, echoes, and the quiet grace of what's left standing.

These days, my hours are filled with everything I wanted—and nothing I expected. I'm an athlete at a desk. A coach in a business suit. A man who once blacked out on bar floors, who now signs off on eight-figure budgets.

And I show up—day in, day out.

I used to think transformation meant becoming someone new. Now I know it means finally becoming who we were meant to be. As an athlete, I could guide maybe a handful of others on my team. As a coach, I could mentor perhaps a hundred a week. In my role, at my desk, with the responsibilities

I've taken on, I oversee the mentoring of over 6,000 kids a week, as well as 100 employees.

Coach Eli said it best: "You didn't just rebuild a life, Daniel. You built a place that keeps other kids from having to fall the same way you did."

He's right. Now I build places for others to land—*safely*. I hug my kids. I lead my team. I provide a place for thousands of kids to get it all out of their system, and I gently weave in my life lessons—just enough for them to stick the landing, but gently enough that they won't notice the coach's hand.

We have a saying at the gym: "Meets don't make champions; *reps* do." I believe this applies when approaching life's transformational changes as well. It worked for me, and I try to run Gyminny Kids with that bigger vision in mind.

We don't build confidence in competition. We build it in repetition.

* * *

One of the daily tasks I do, religiously, is close-up at night. During the day, the gyms are filled with a cacophony of noise. It's the most joyful sound you have ever heard. And there's a cadence to the day, starting gently with the morning preschool mom-and-me classes, then the early afternoon tots, the mid-afternoon invasion of school kids, and later, the more focused efforts of competitive teens. After that, there's the wind-down of thank-yous and byes, and see-you-tomorrows, from the last remaining staff. Finally, the day ends with the almost meditative quiet of the team finishing up and leaving. After that, I love to walk around whichever location I'm at, just checking stuff, tugging at the parallel bars, and even taking off my shoes and socks and jumping up on the beam.

When I was younger, the pommel horse was my avatar. It demanded constant motion to avoid collapse. There was no room for stillness—just rhythm and showboating. If I stopped moving, I fell—so I learned to keep spinning. Steve Butcher used to say you didn't fall off the pommel horse because you made a technical mistake; you fell because you lost focus. The underlying message I've taken away is to trust our training, don't overthink it, and learn how to create a mental routine that's strong enough to keep us from losing focus.

But now? Now I think more about the beam. Nobody trained me for it—it's not part of the men's program. But life doesn't care about your program, and I've been teaching it for over 20 years. On the beam, we either learn to balance or we fall. I've often compared the rhythm needed on the beam to rolling a penny down a hill; as long as the momentum is moving forward, there tends to be little to no wobbles, but as soon as the penny starts to slow down, it shakes and falls over. We have to keep the routine moving confidently.

My youth was more like losing focus on the horse.

These days, I've found balance and focus.

And often, as I take in the quiet, zen-like stillness of the empty gym, the final rays of the San Diego sunset will trace golden beams through the darkening air. And when they do, they always give me pause.

I'm a man of faith. I've kept that information out of my *addiction* story, but as it is a more tangible part of my personal *recovery* story, I think now is a fair time to mention it. And when I look at those golden beams, I contemplate the bigger picture. The day I walk barefoot up those beams, I want to do so with balance and poise. I want to look back and know I walked that beam with purpose.

And every now and then, in that last hush before I leave, I remember the morning Finley found me—face down on the carpet, bathed in golden light.

That day, she asked me—without knowing it—to find my purpose.

And these evenings remind me: I did.

I have two final "rituals" in my evening routine before I head home.

The first is to tap on the changing room doors as I walk towards the main exit. It's my way of reminding myself that, no matter who or what we are, there will always be room for change.

And the very last thing I do before closing the door at night is look back into the dark and say:

"Good night, baby gorilla; sweet dreams."

Baby Gorilla

Working My Way Back

With a student, Gyminny Kids, San Diego, CA.

Coaching my youngest son, Rocket.

Gyminny Kids Inc. 5000 honoree.

Check presentation, at Rady Children's
Hospital, San Diego, CA.

With my Baby Gorilla, San Diego,
CA.

The family I never thought I'd live
to see.

These days, if I showboat, it's for the kids.

144

The Early Days

Warming up on the pommel horse.

Laguna Beach, CA.

The car wreck, San Diego, CA.

The LA Daze

Backstage at the LA Fashion Week.

Hanging with Pink at the Roosevelt
Hotel shoot (before I got banned).

With David Neuman and friends, no idea
where or when.

www.ingramcontent.com/pod-product-compliance
Lightning Source LLC
Chambersburg PA
CBHW061806120626
46550CB00005B/2166